Dutch Swear Word Coloring Book

By: Shazza T. Jones

Introduction

Learn some Dutch swear words while you sit back and color the pages.

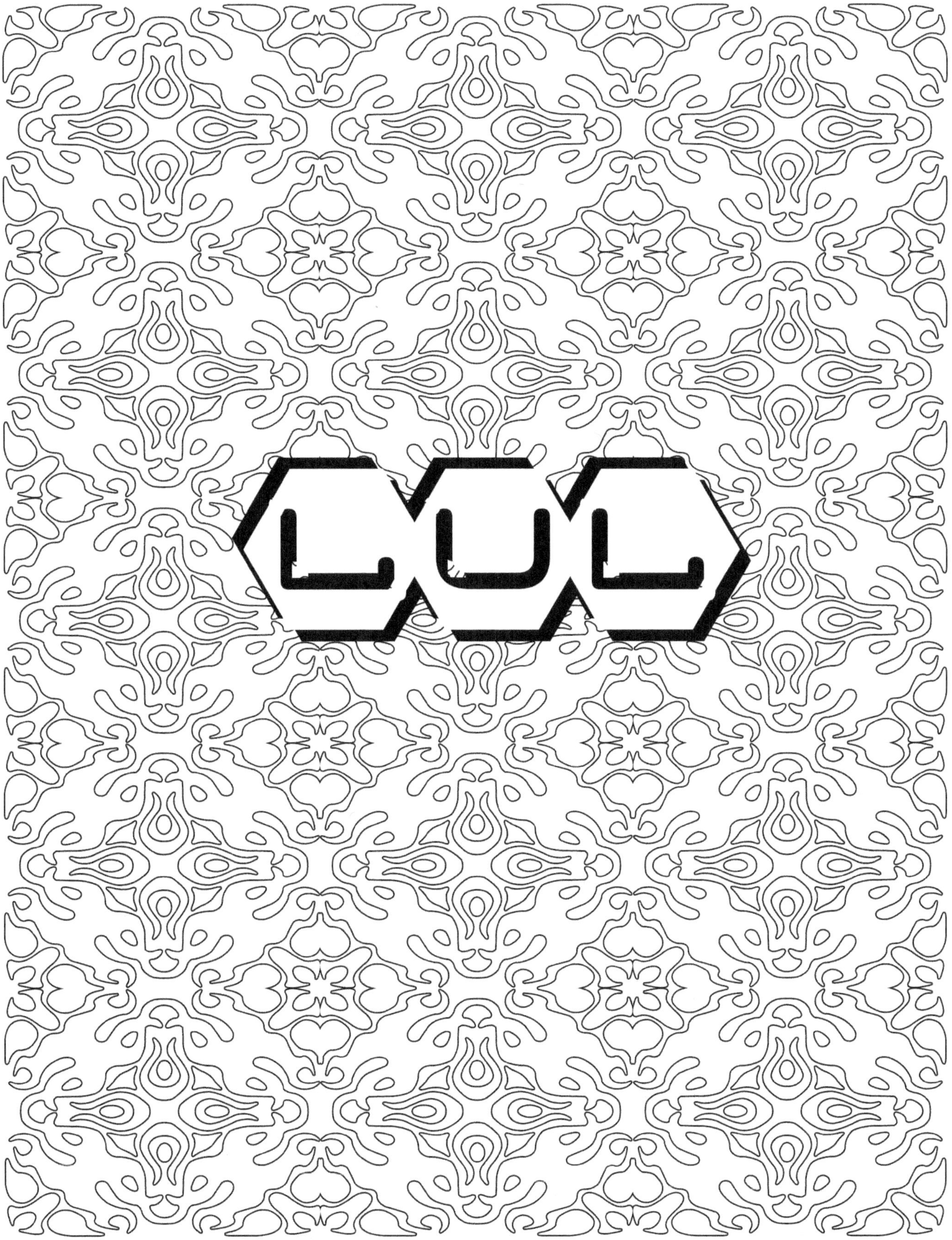
LUL

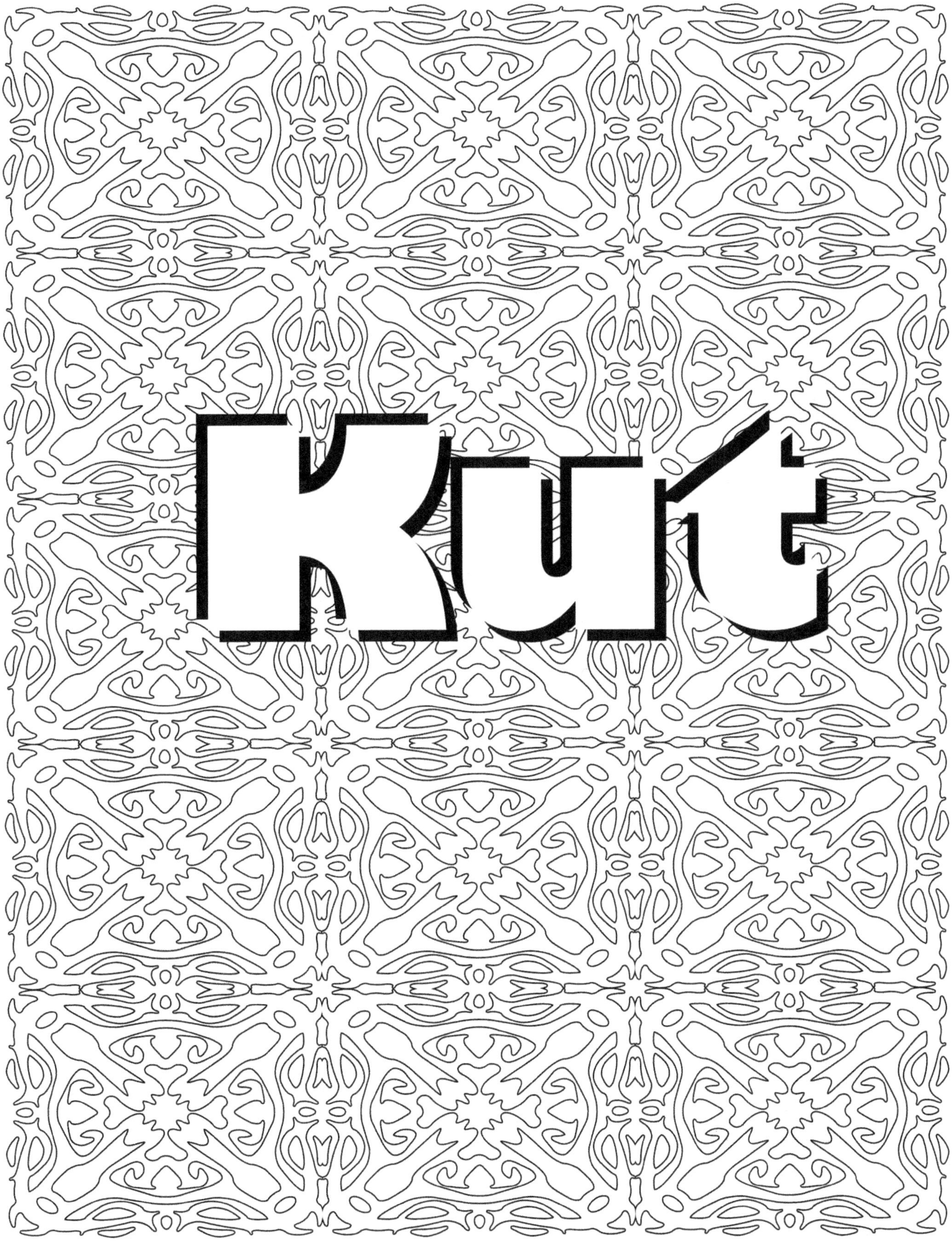
Kut

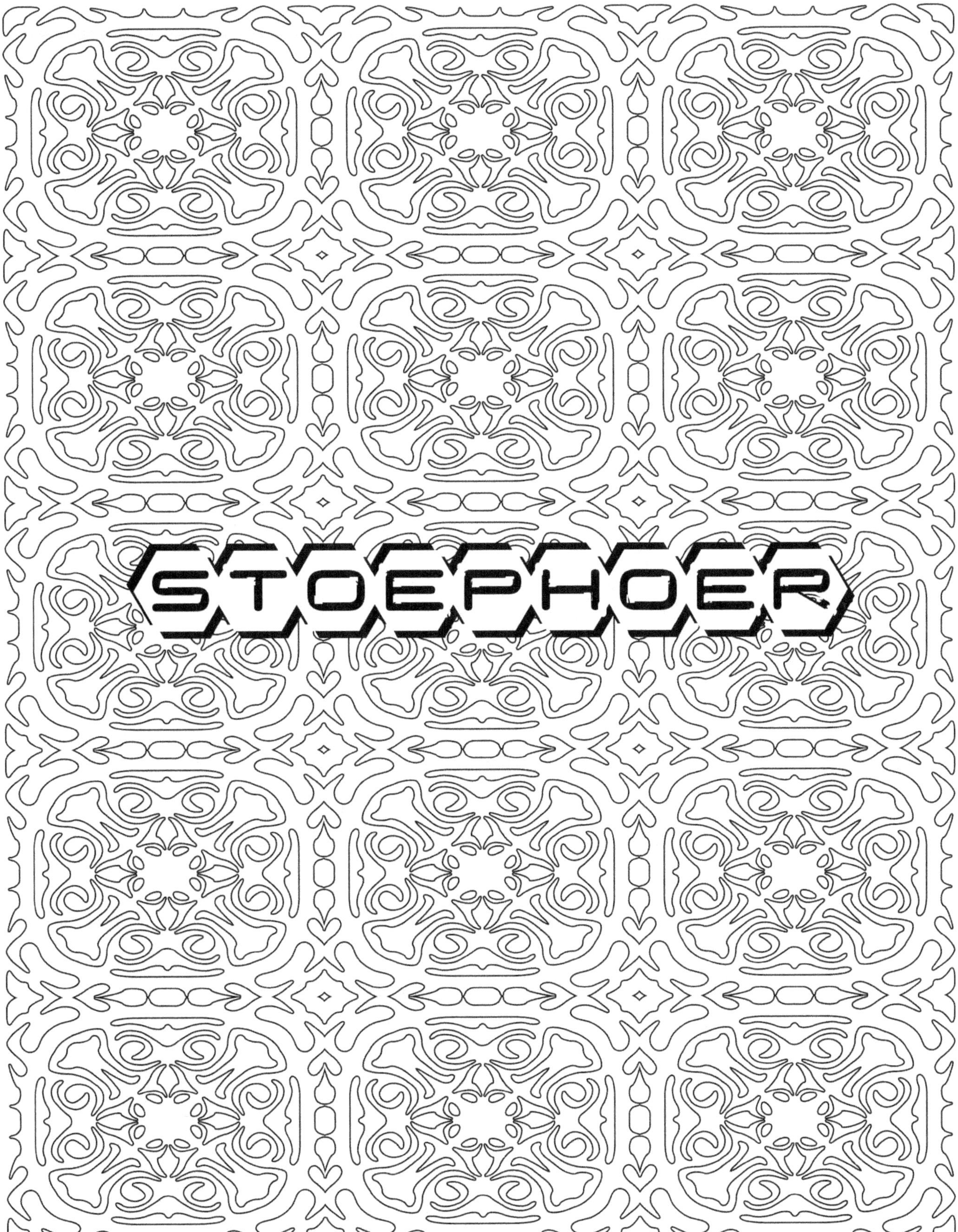
STOEPHOER

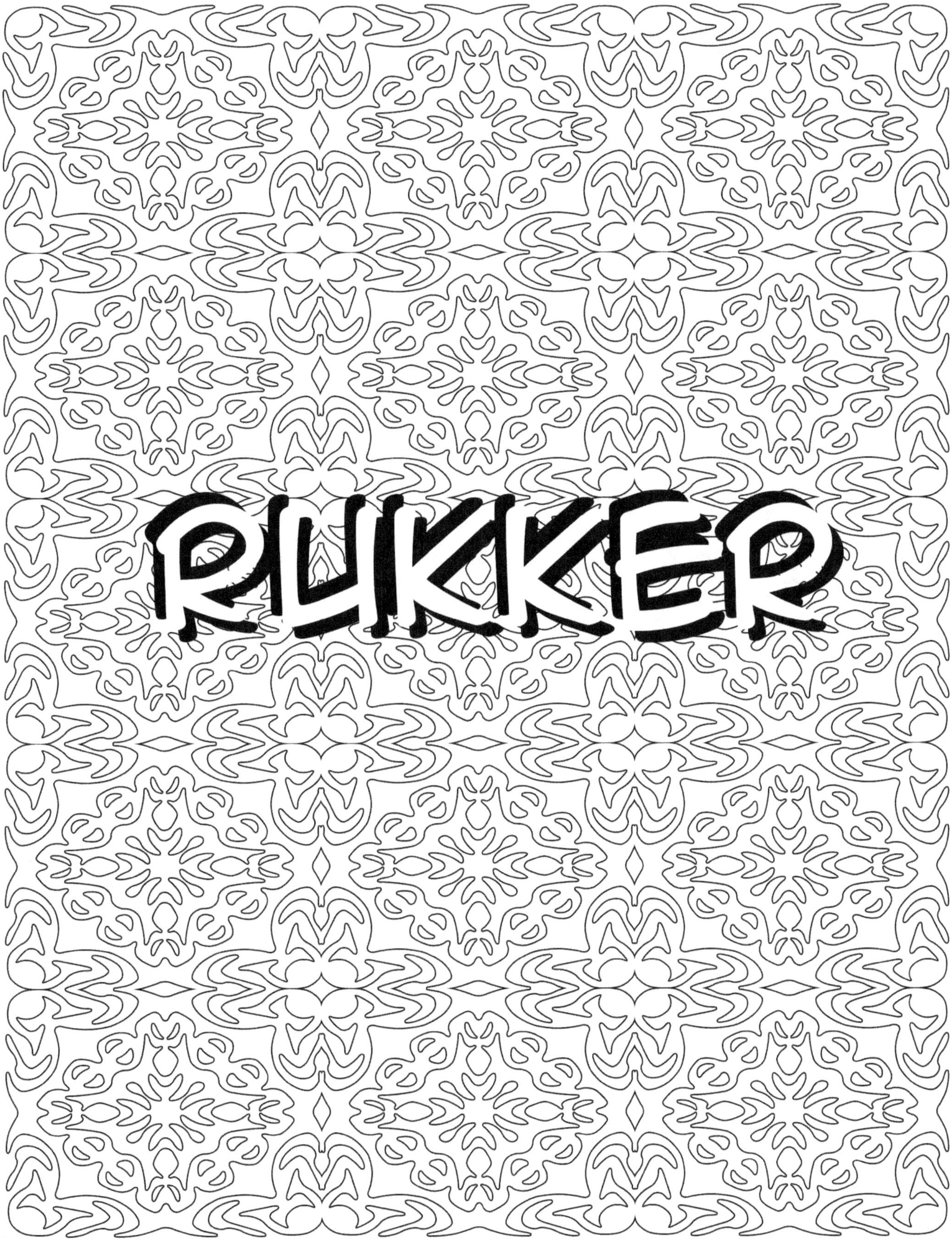
RUKKER

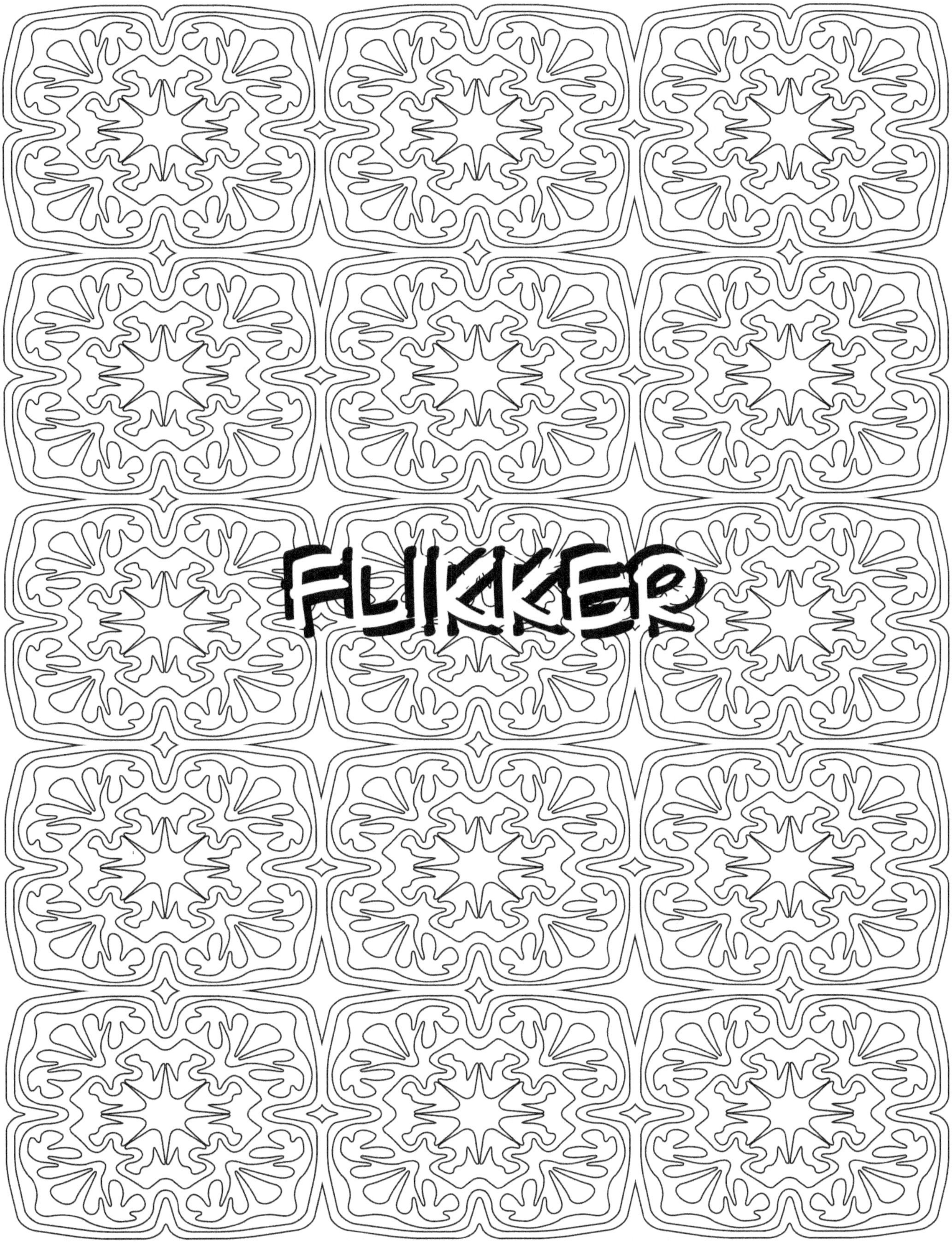
FLIKKER

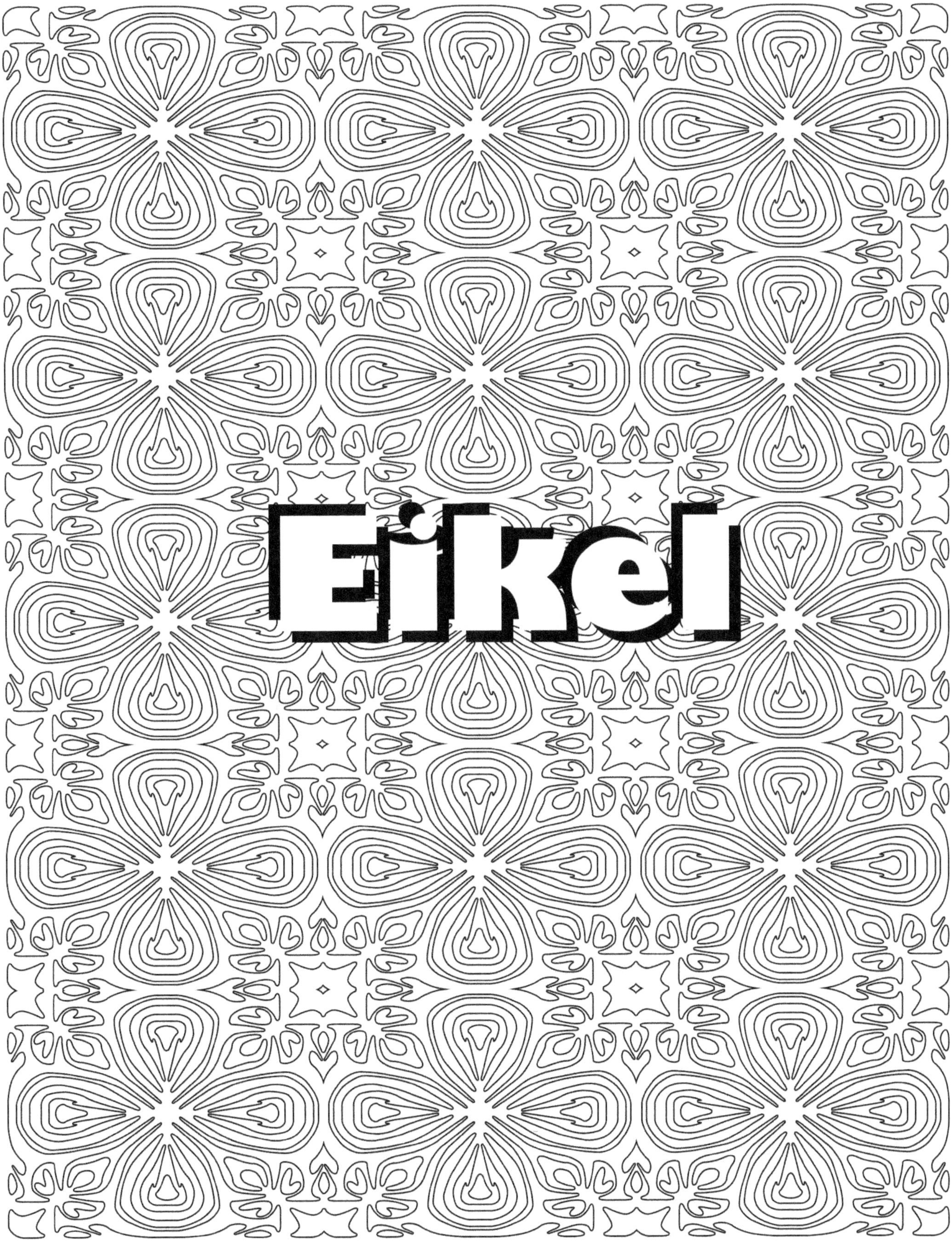
Eikel

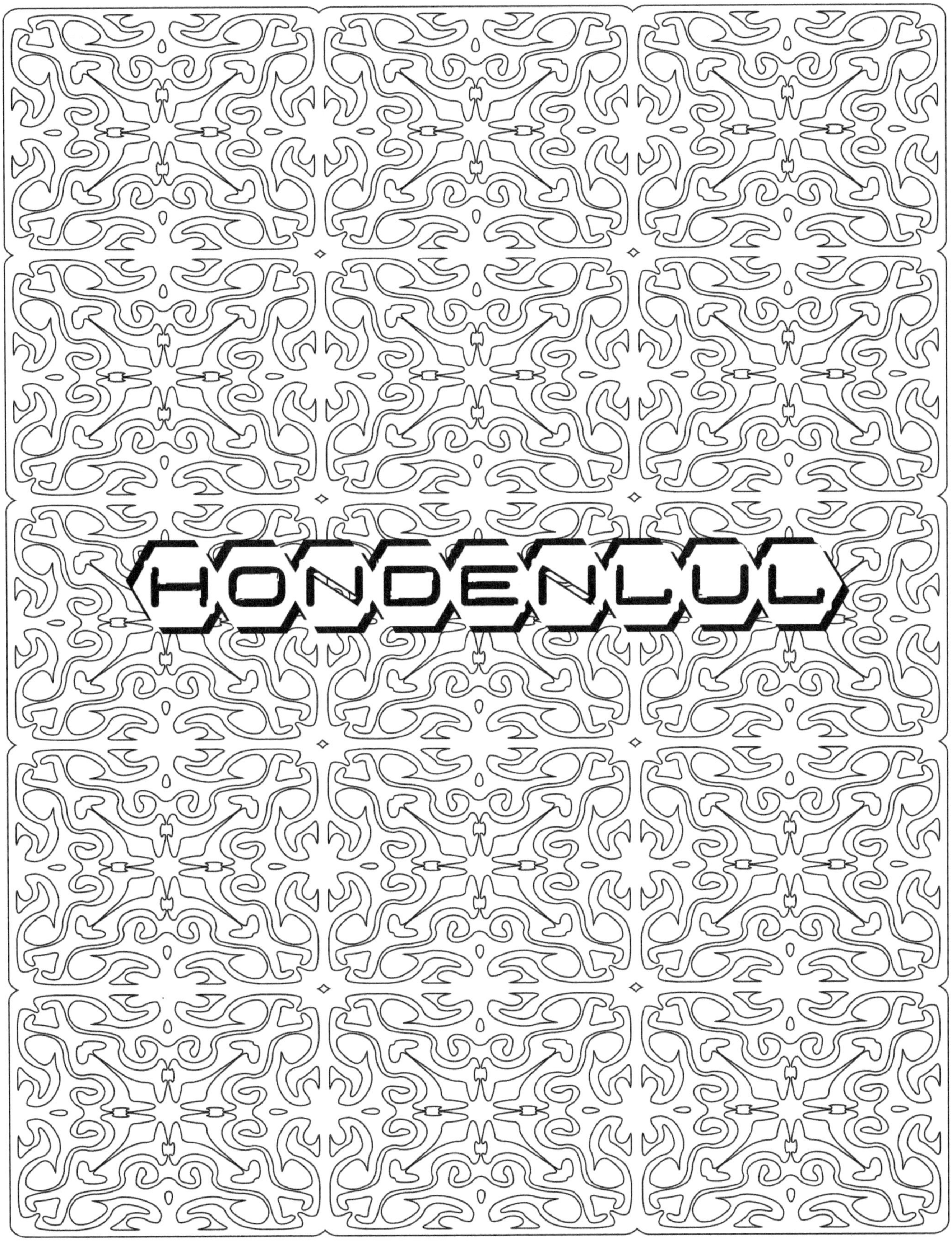
HONDENLUL

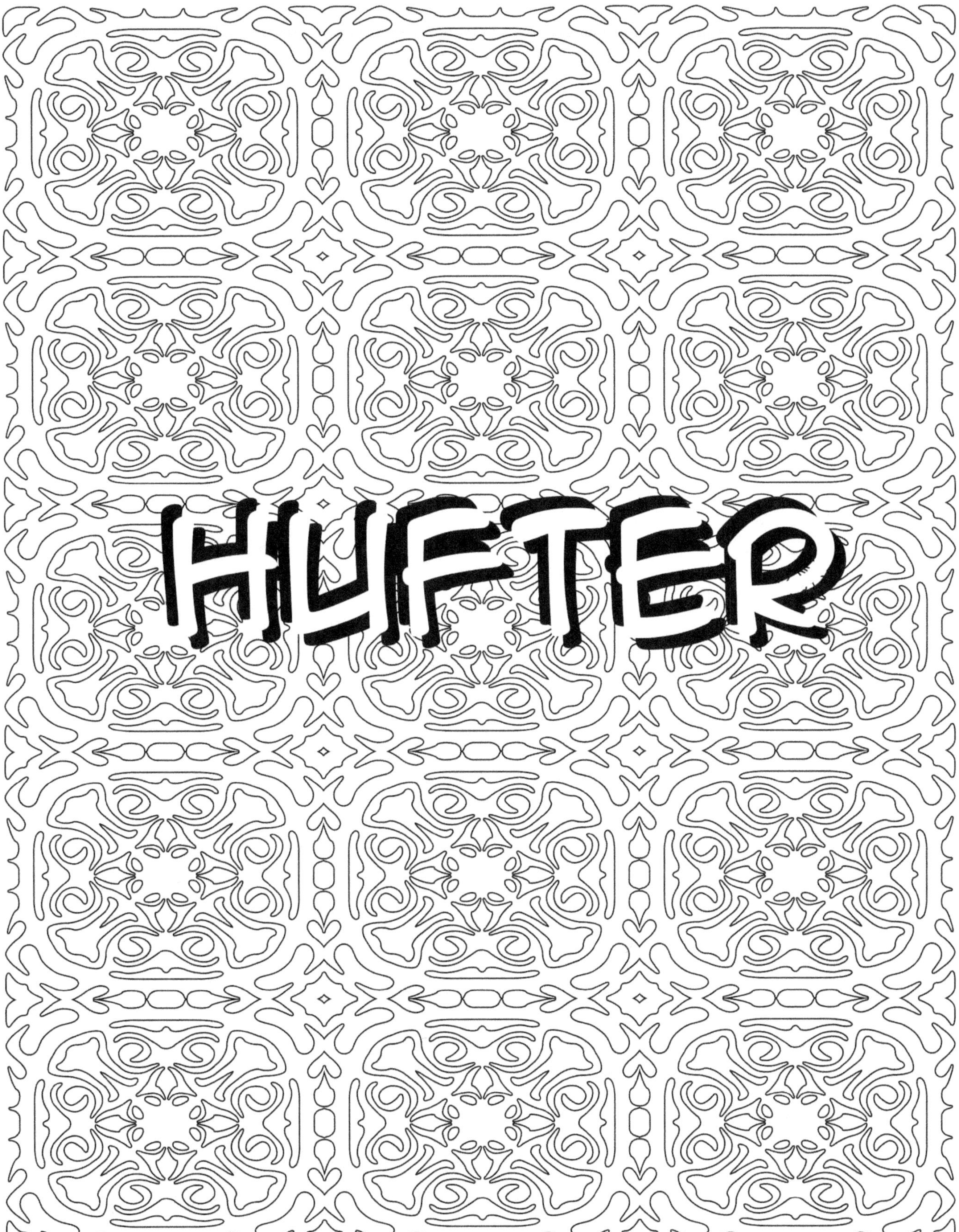
HUFTER

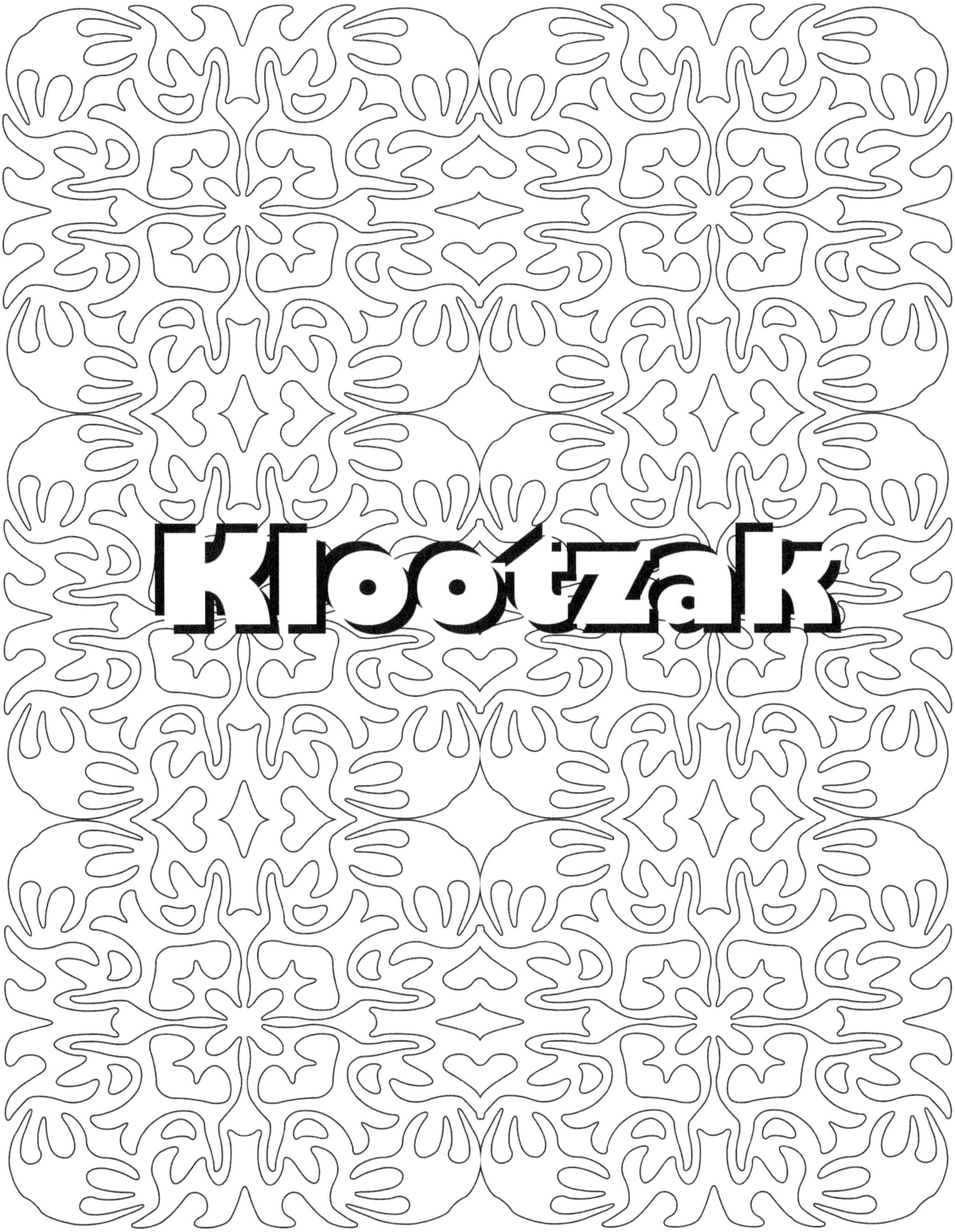
Klootzak

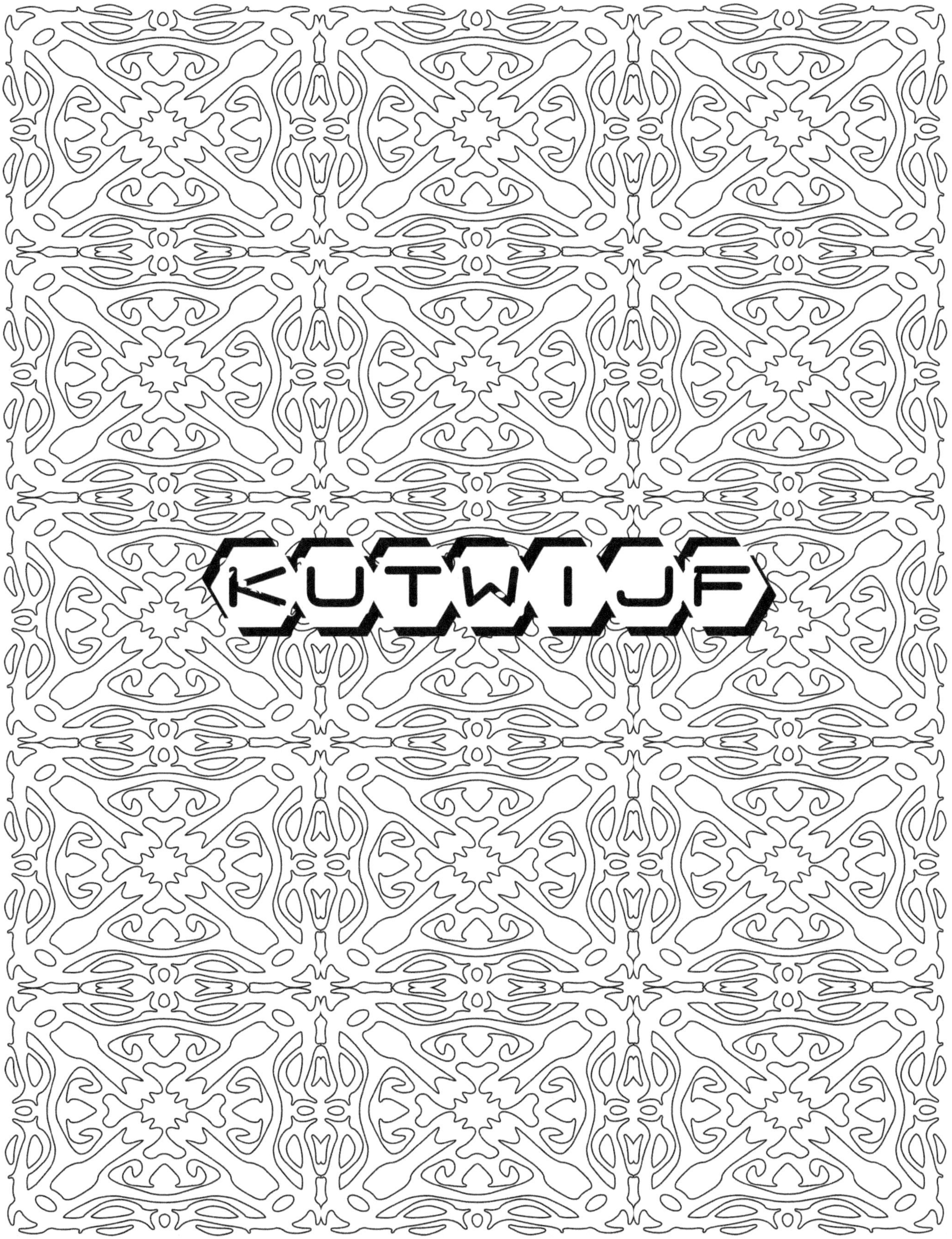
KUTWIJF

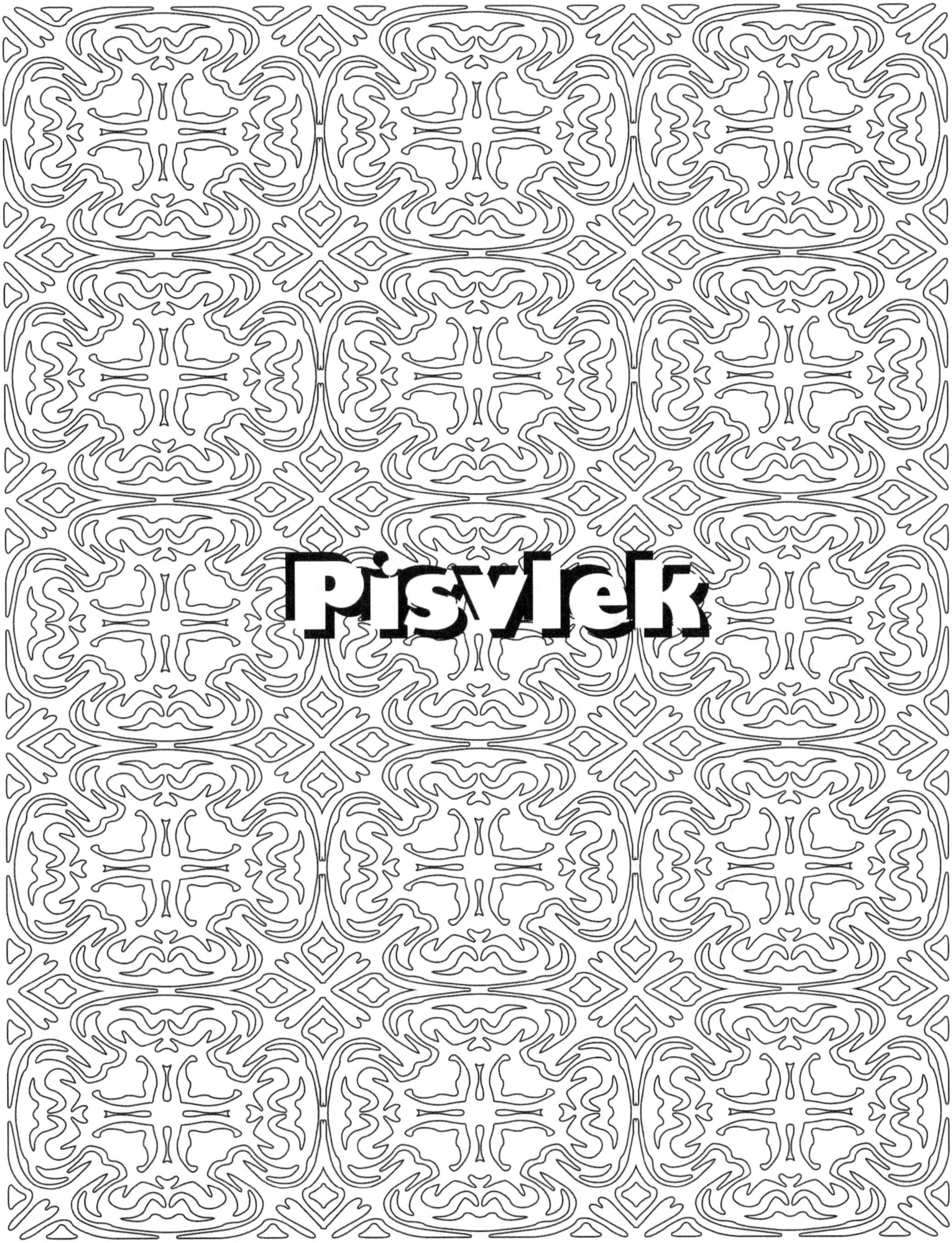
Pisvlek

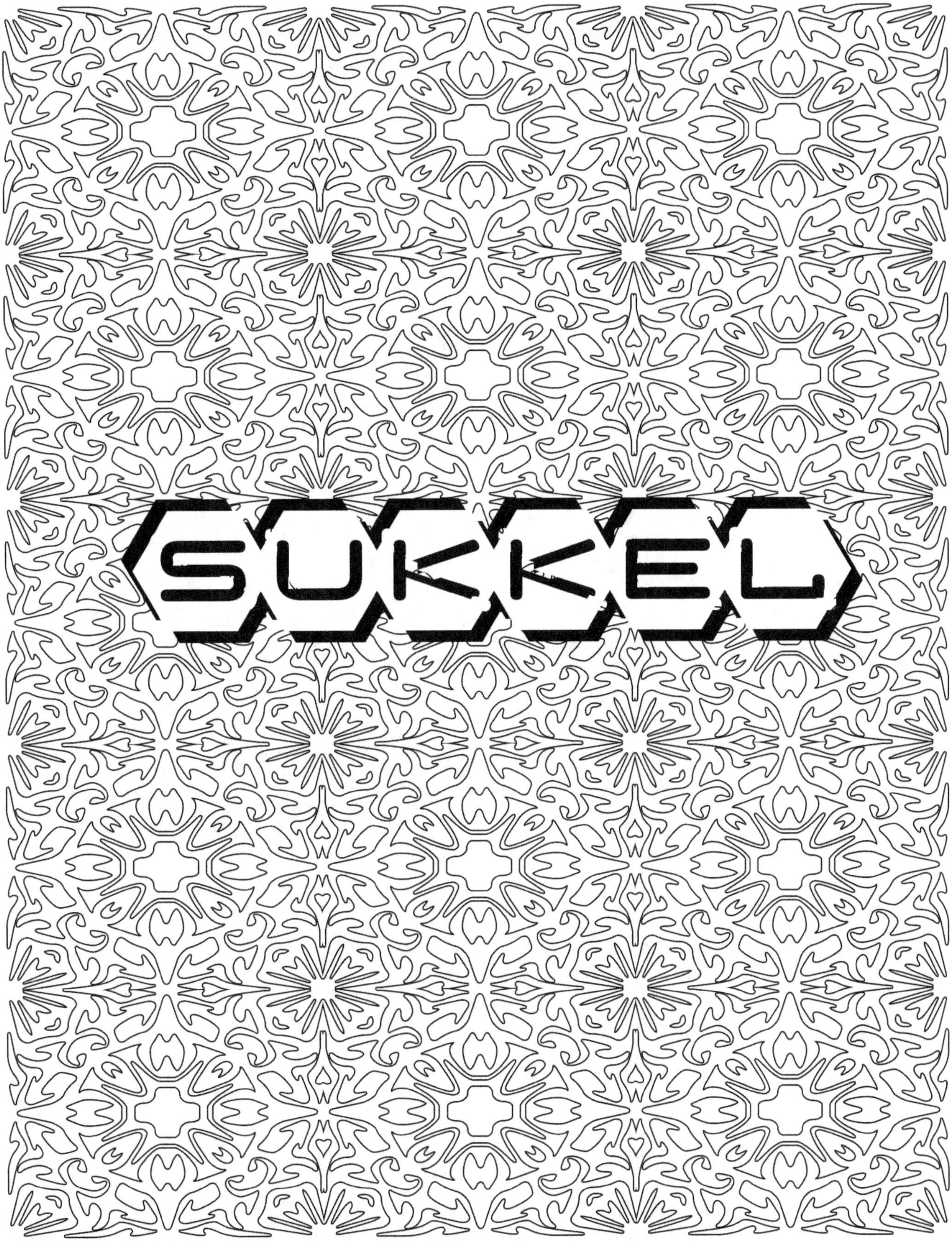
SUKKEL

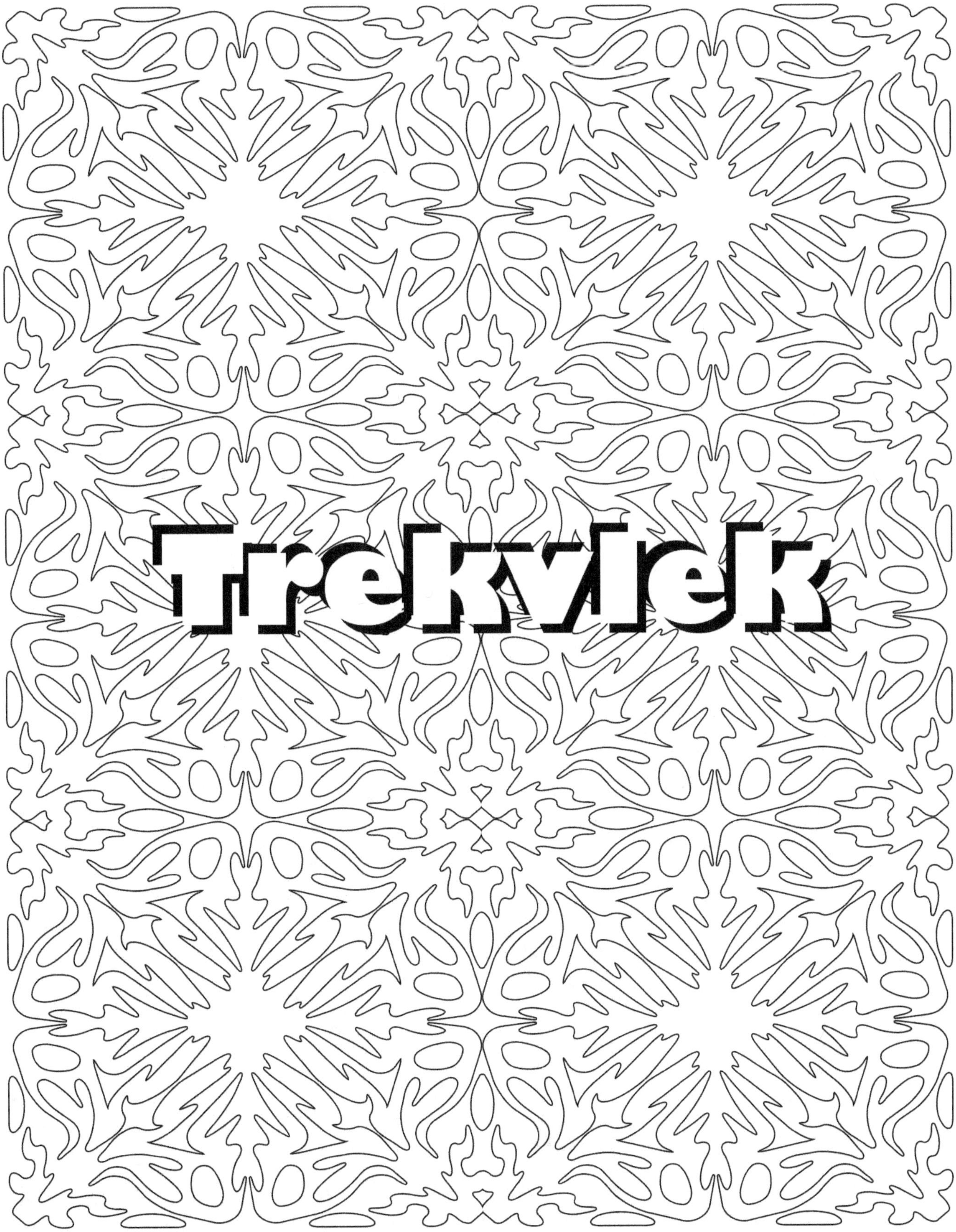
Trekvlek

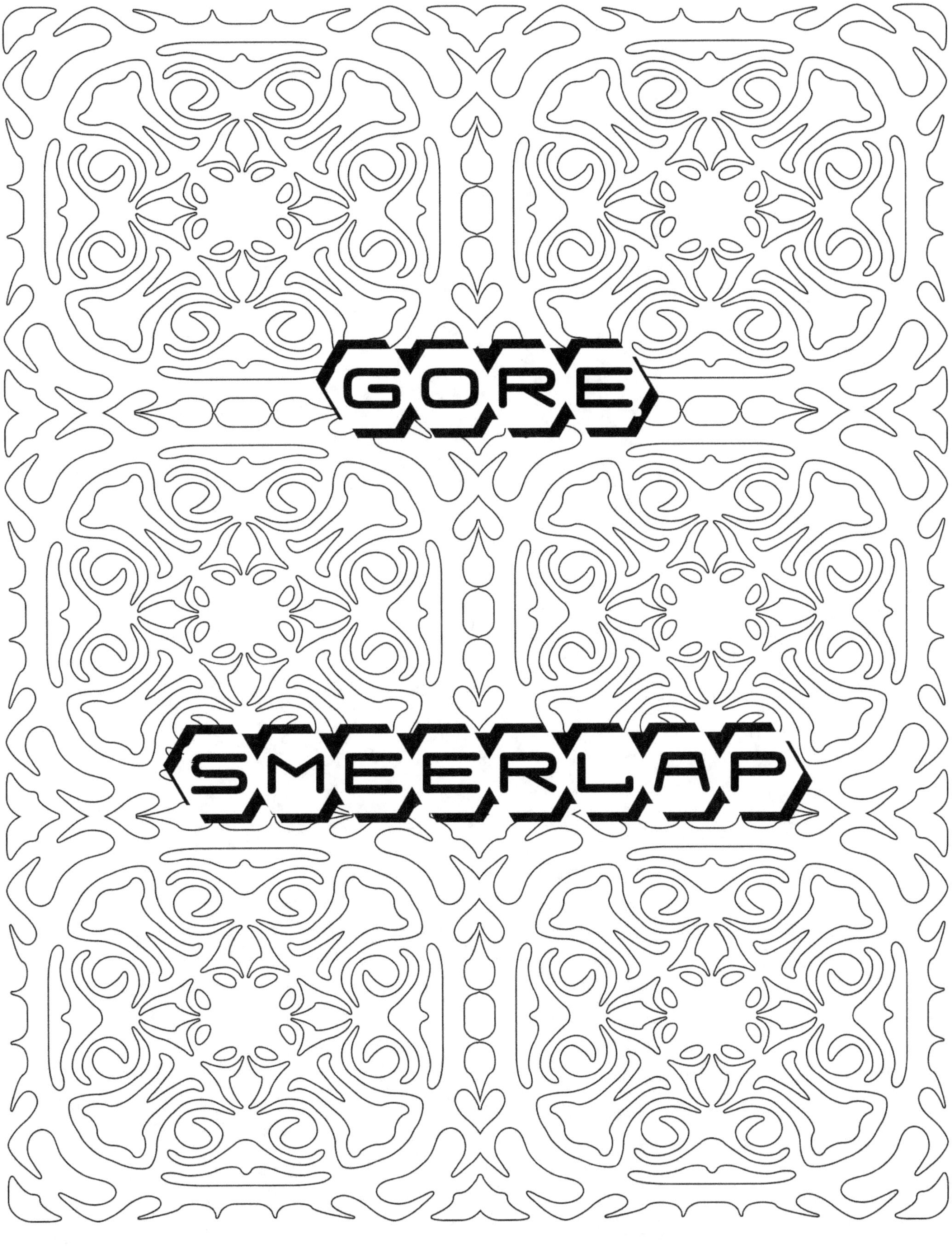
GORE
SMEERLAP

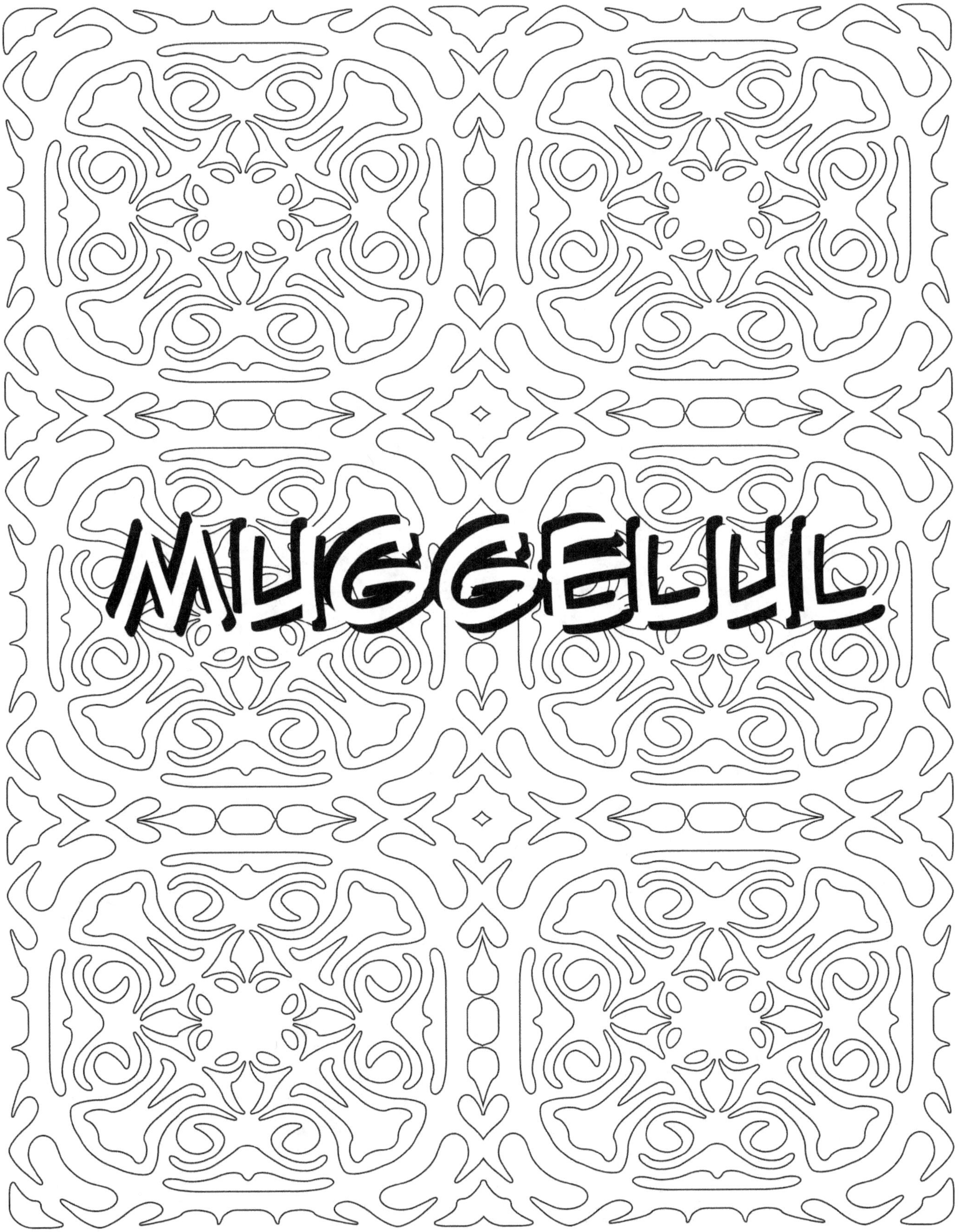
MUGGELUUL

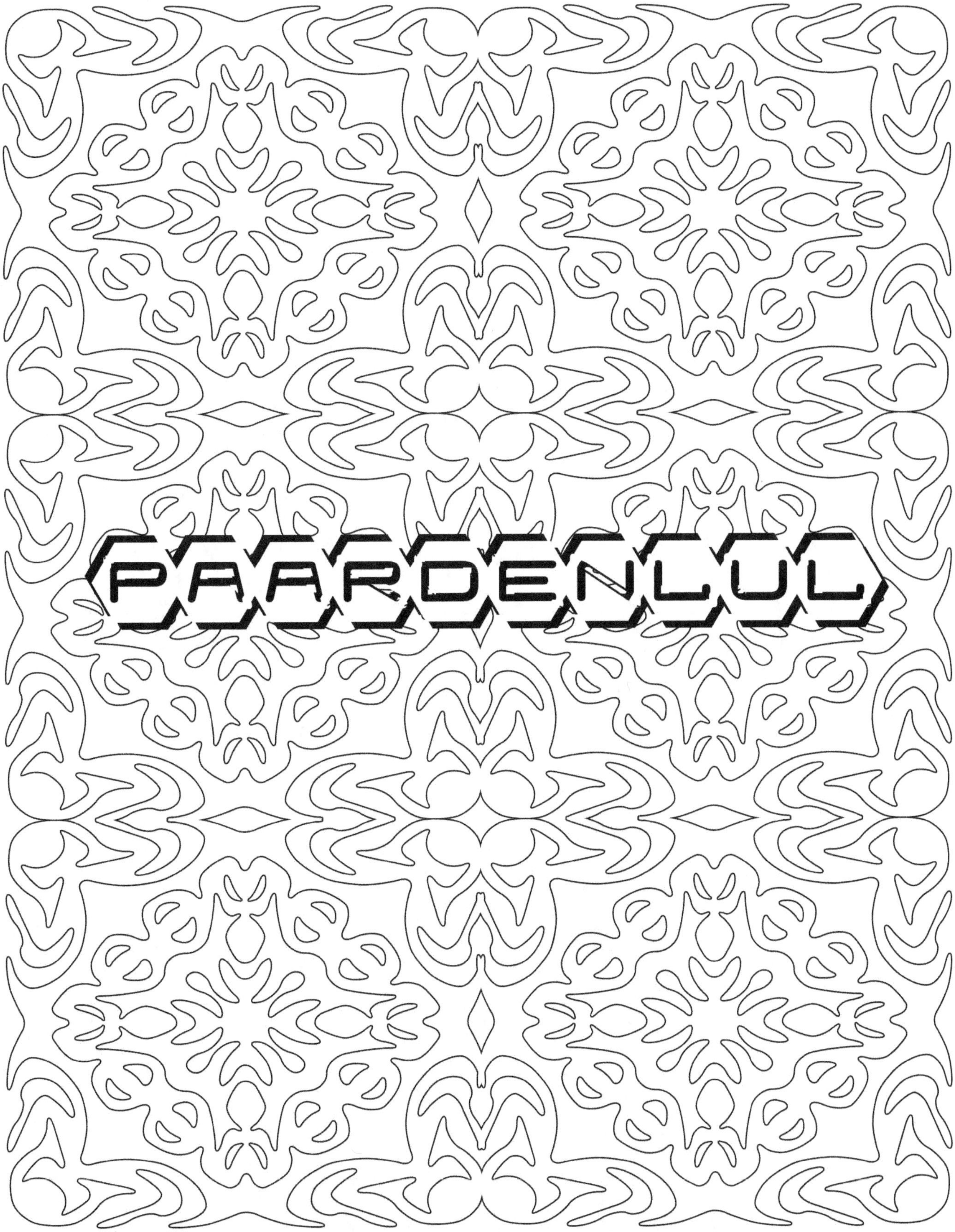
PAARDENLUL

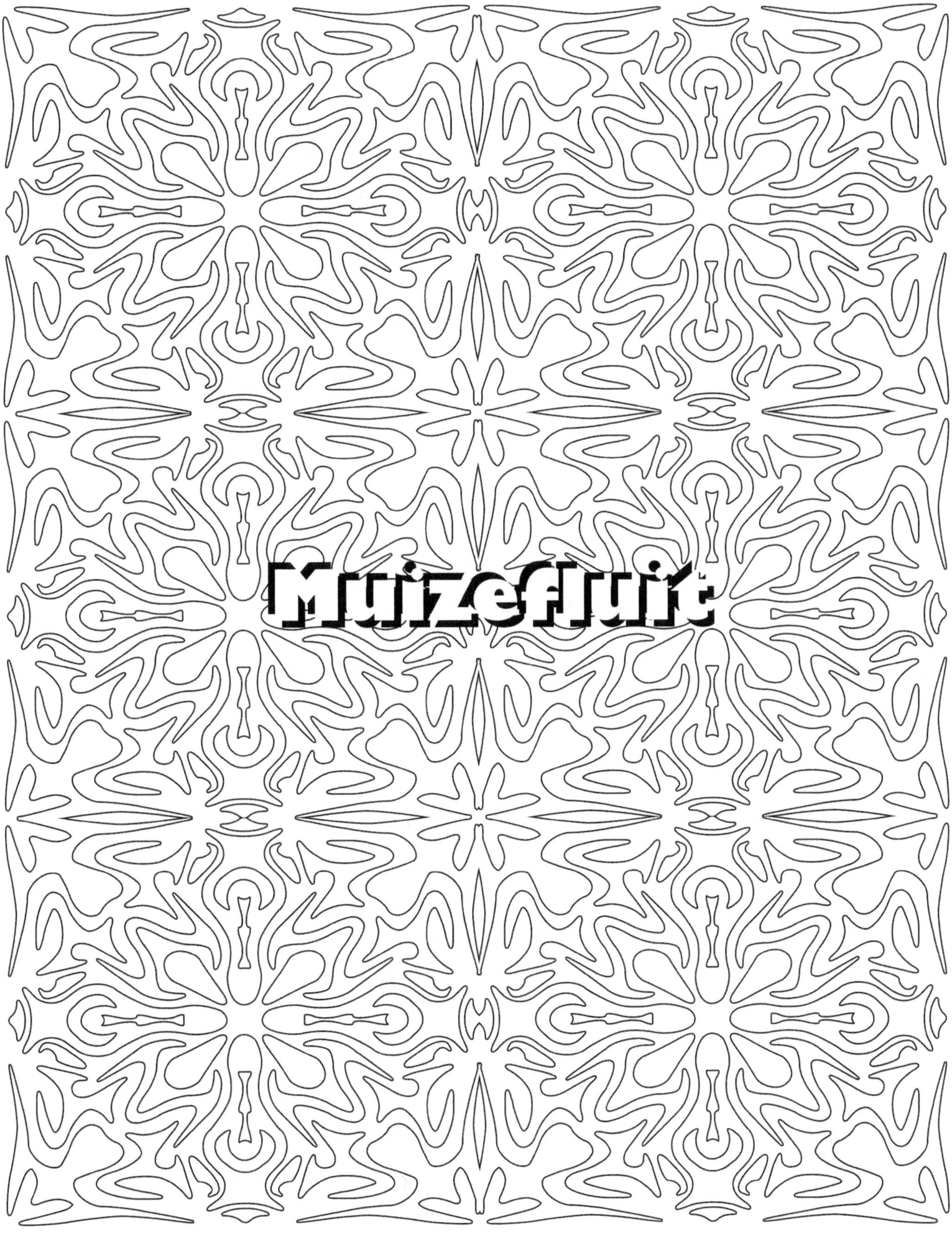
Muizefluit

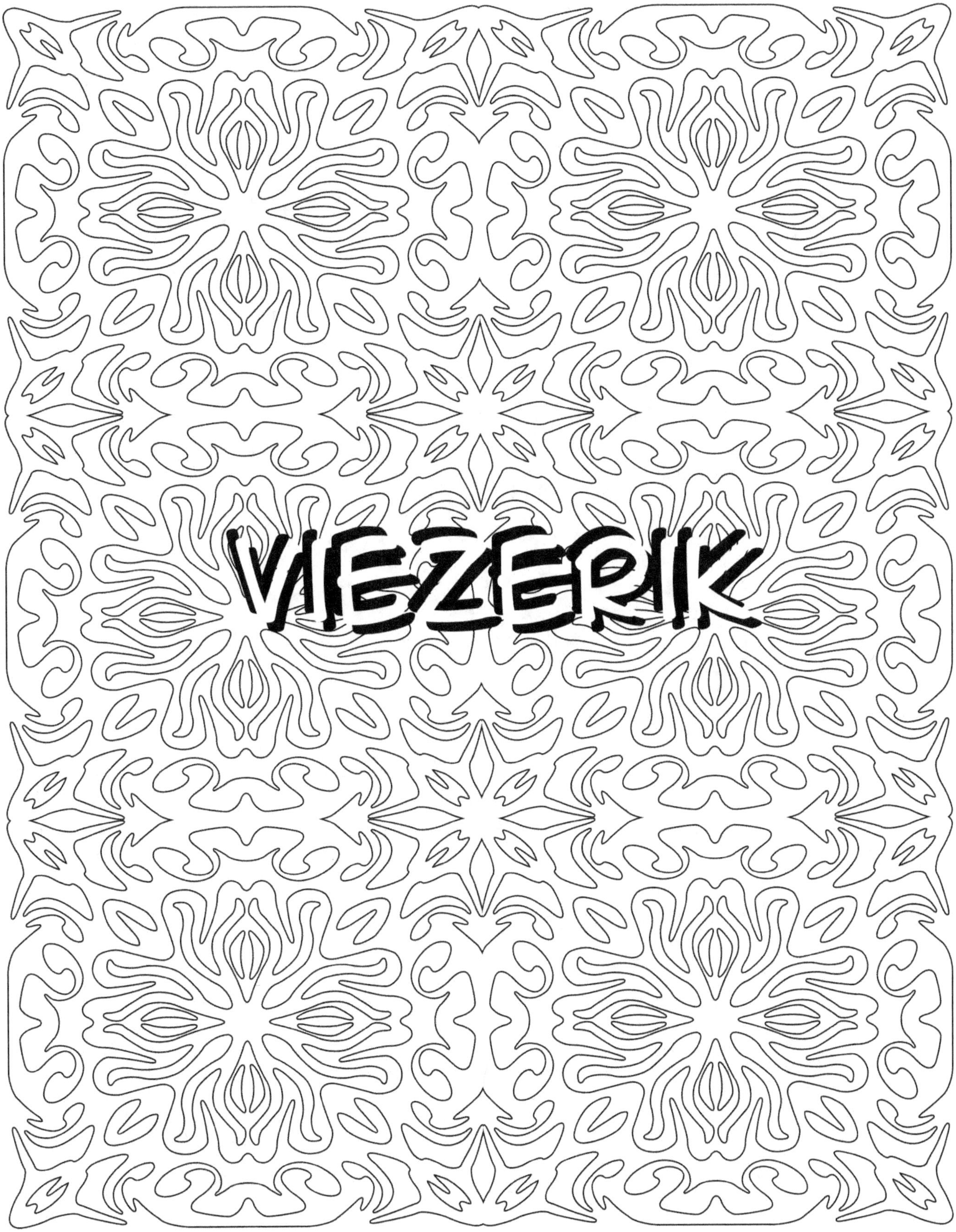
VIEZERIK

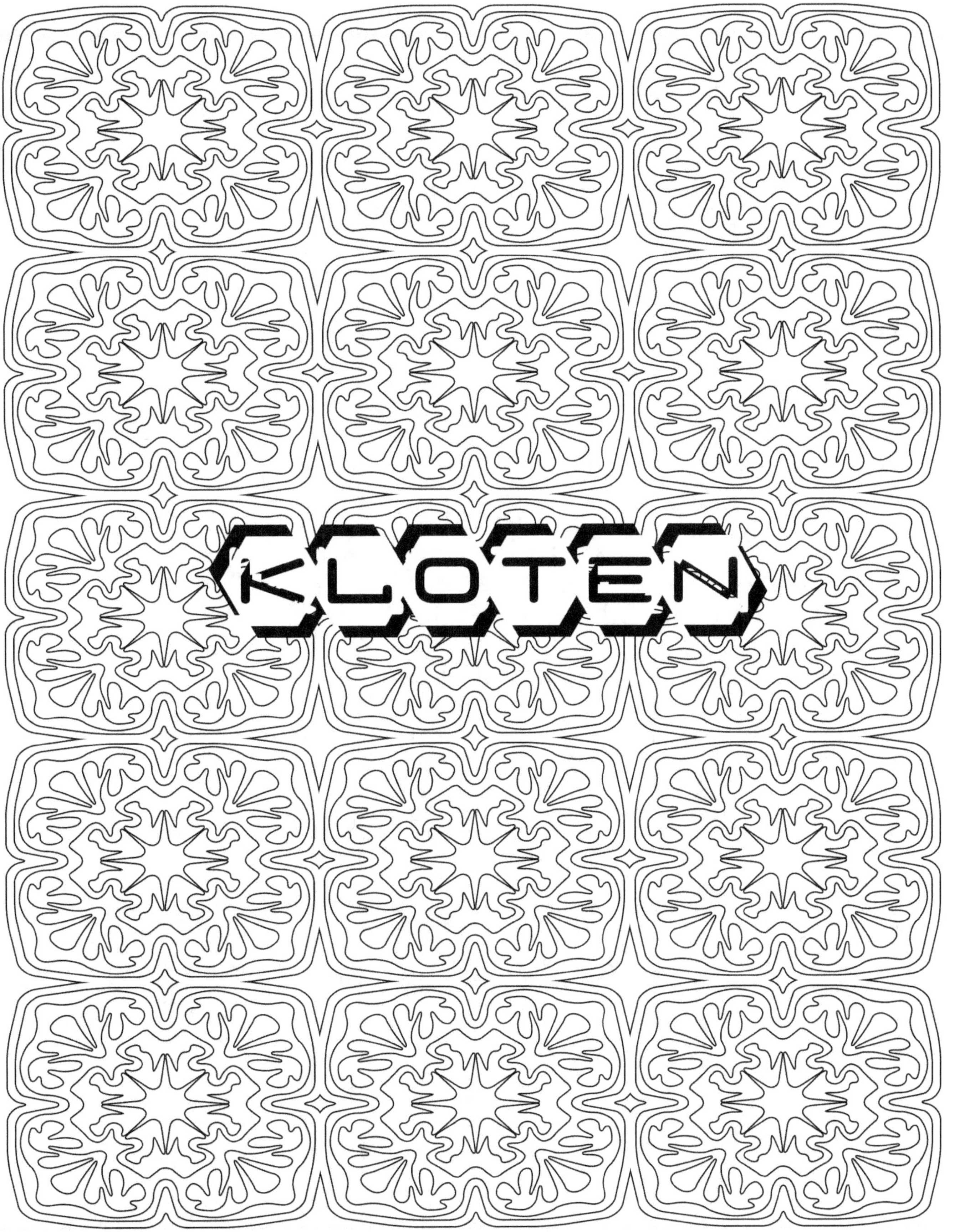
KLOTEN

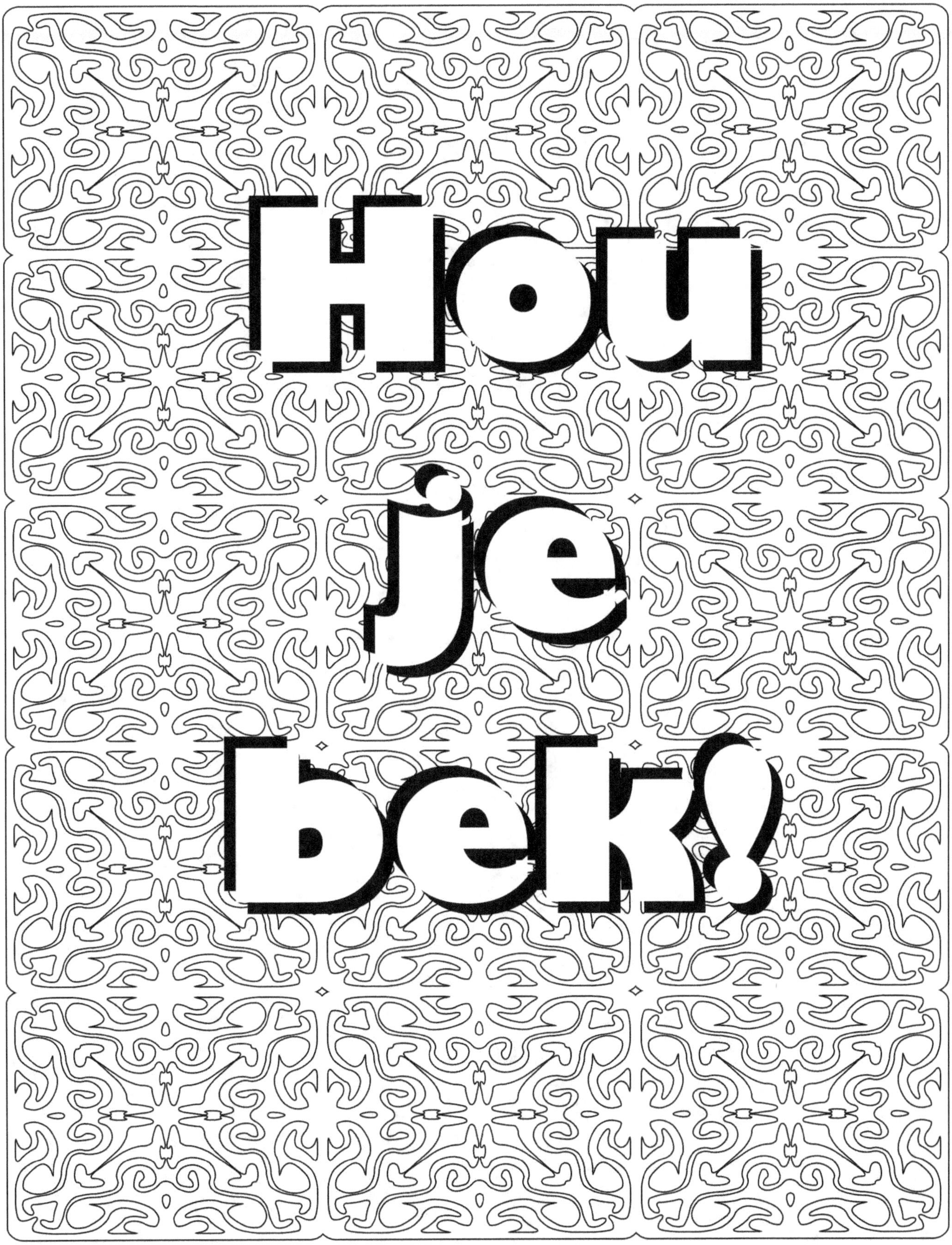
Hou
je
bek!

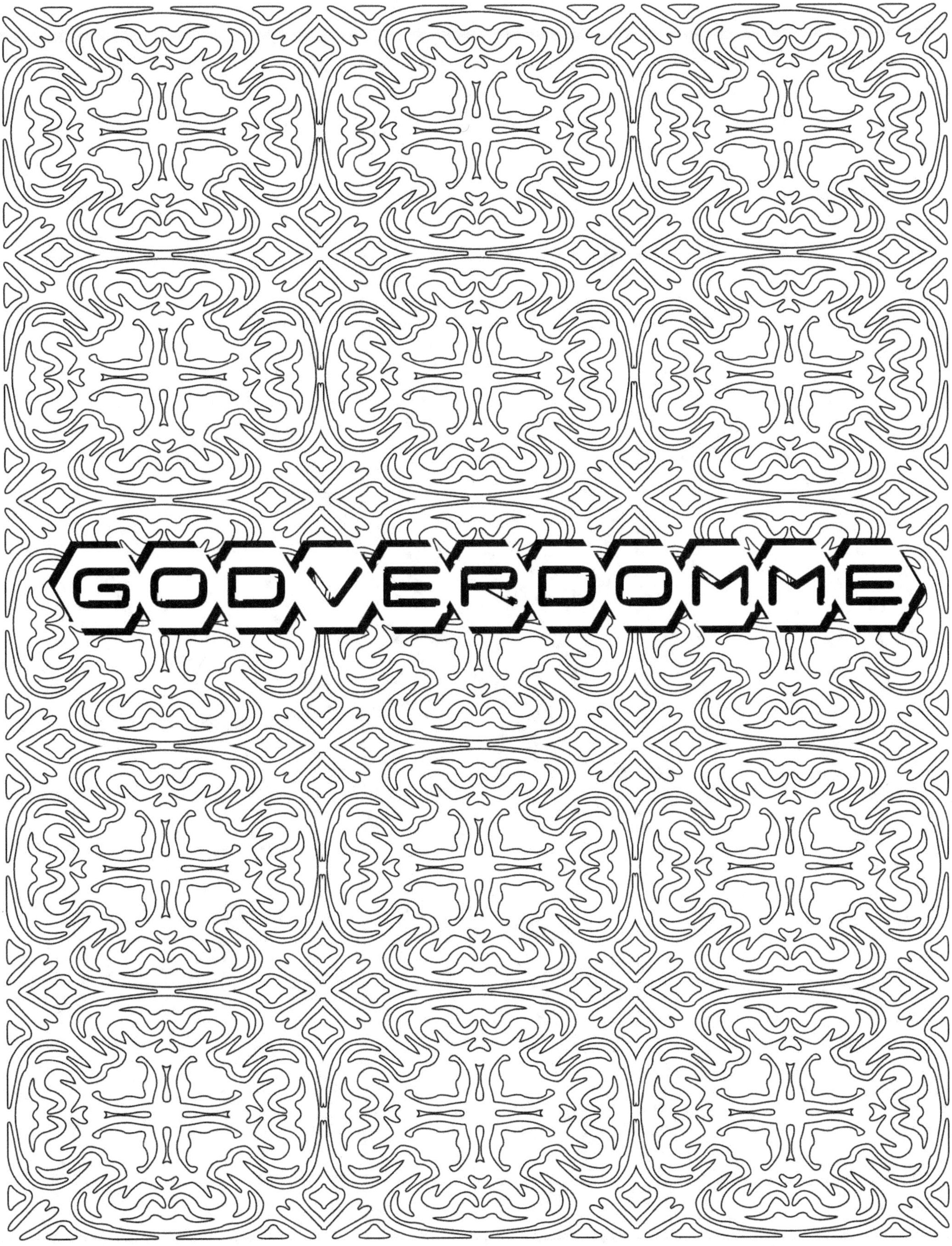
GODVERDOMME

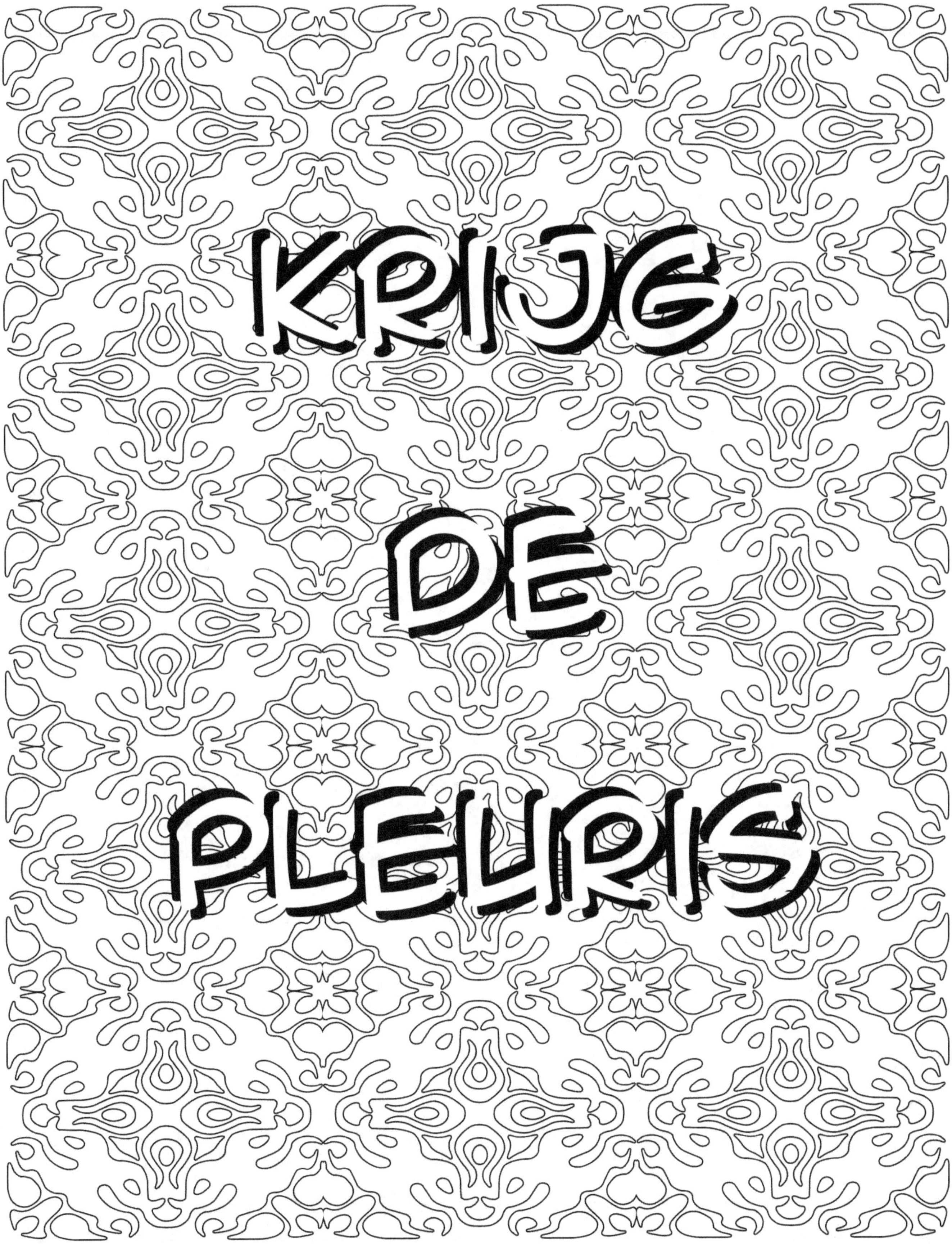
KRIJG
DE
PLEURIS

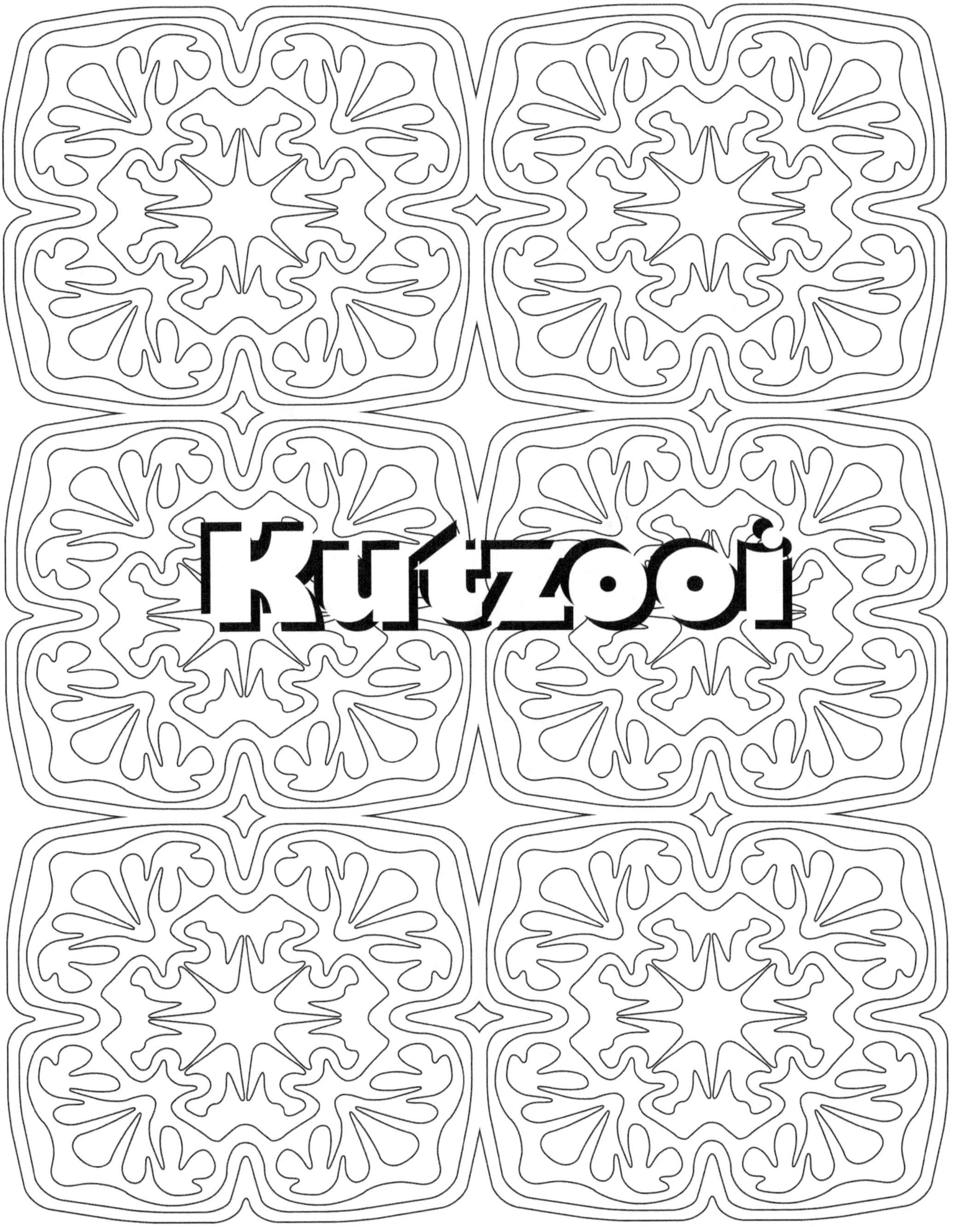
Kutzooi

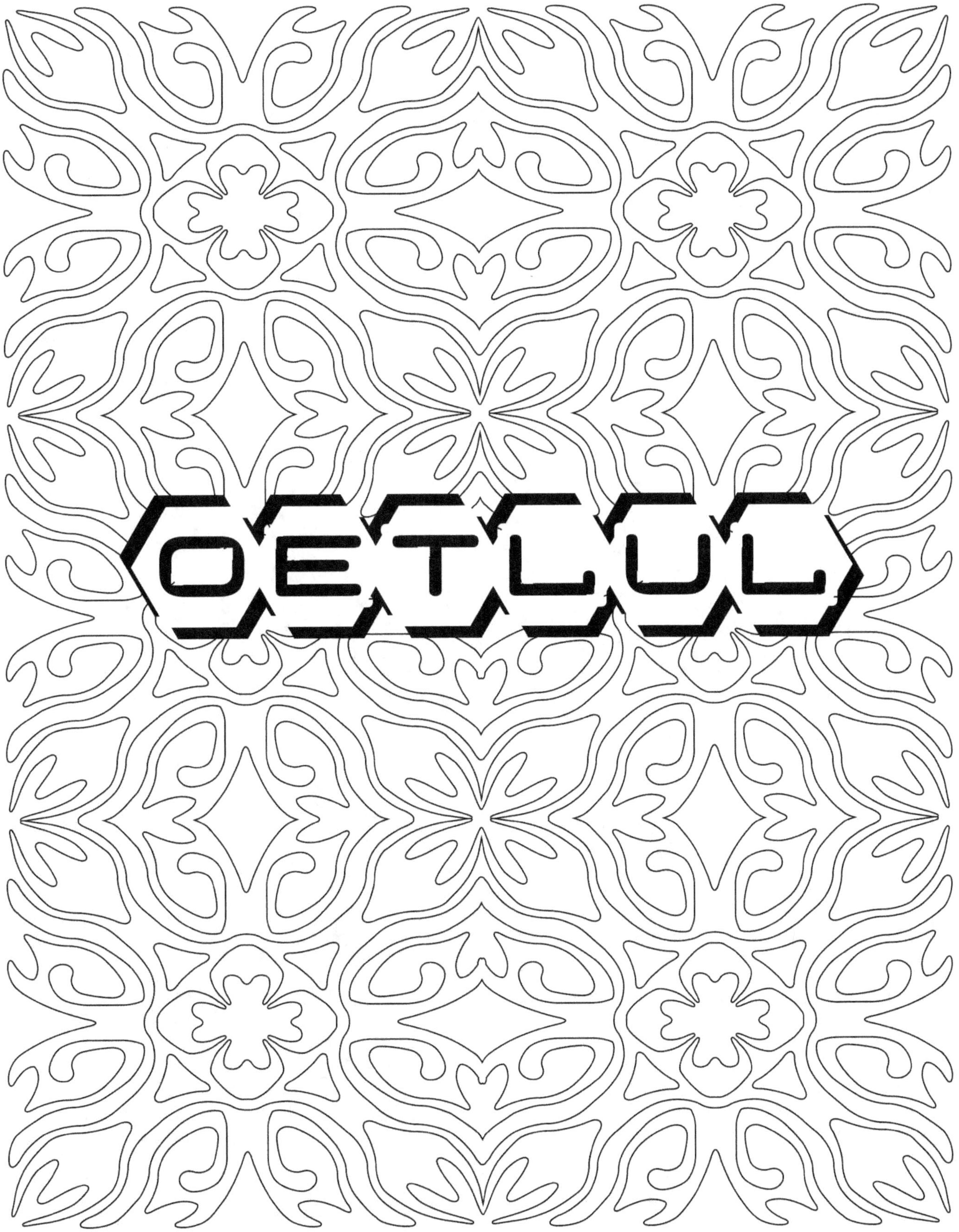
OETLUL

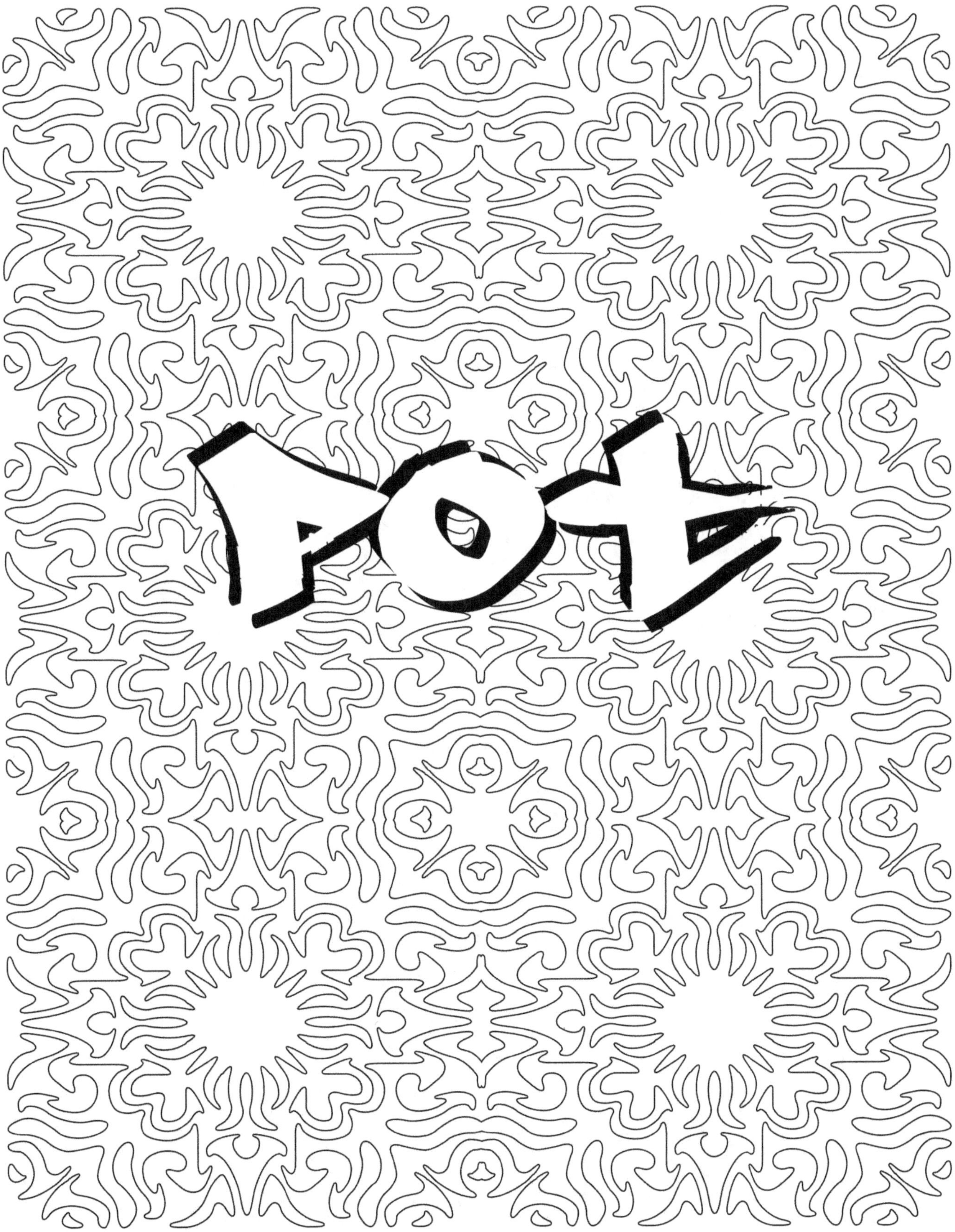

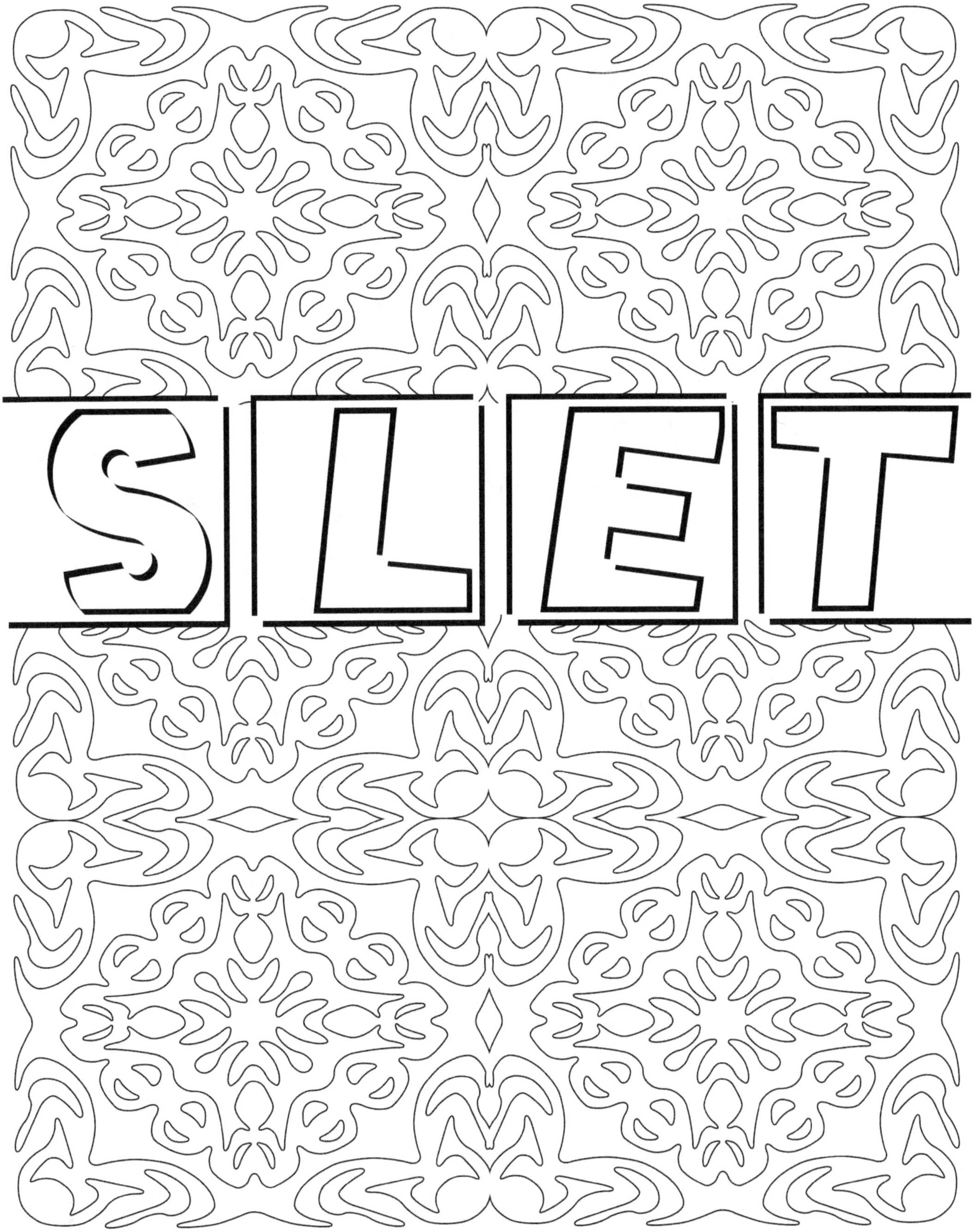
SLET

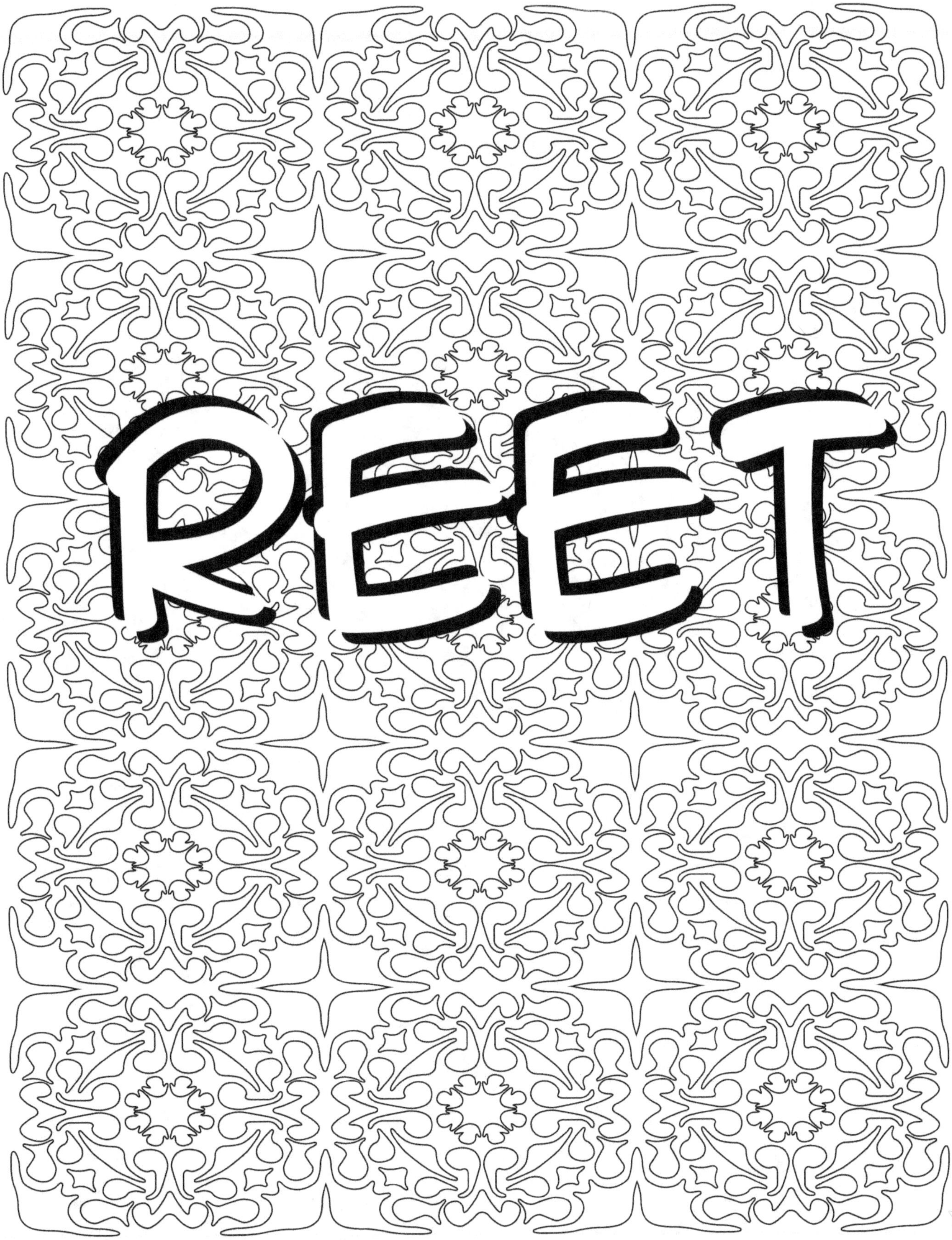
REET

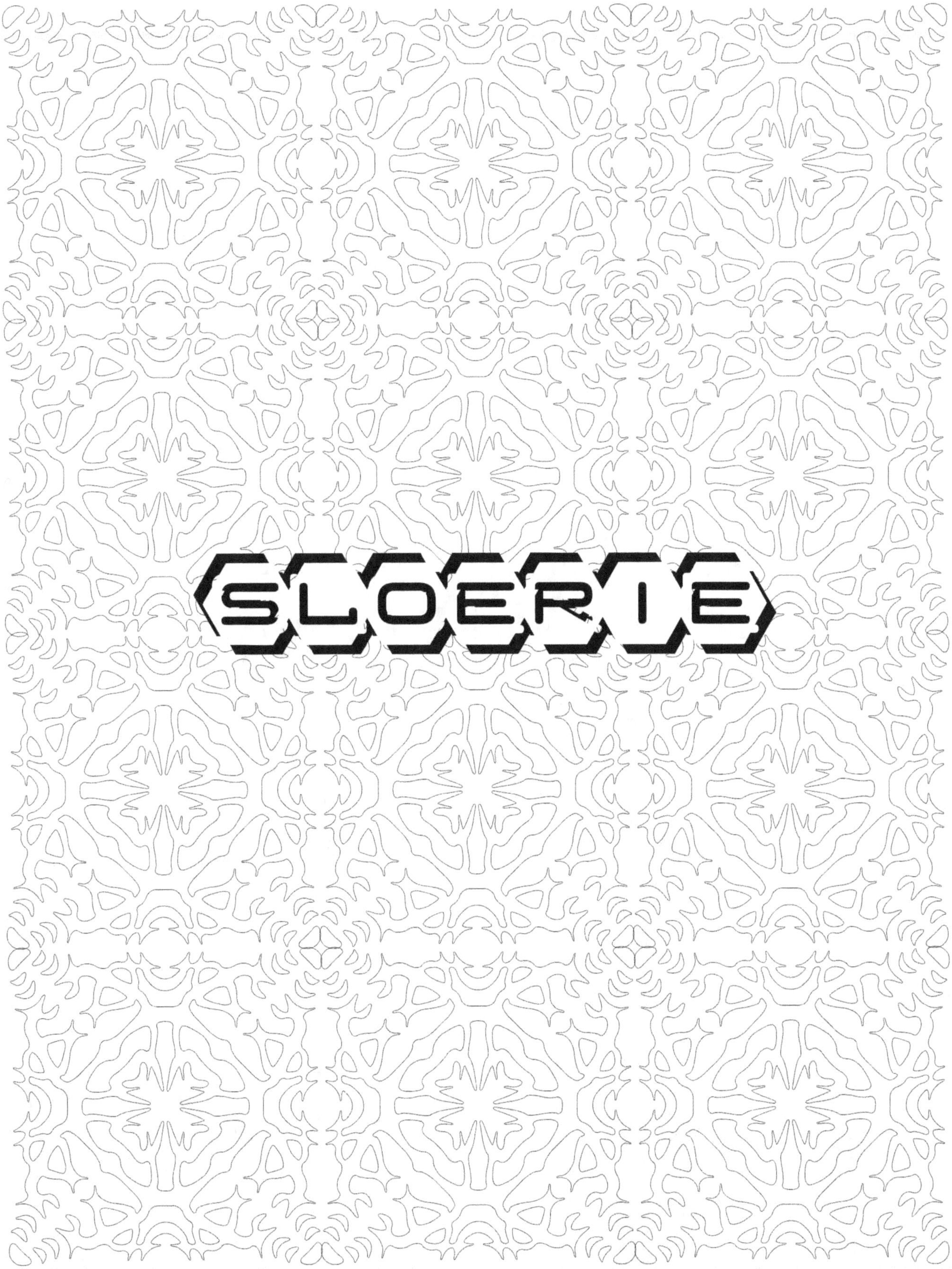
SLOERIE

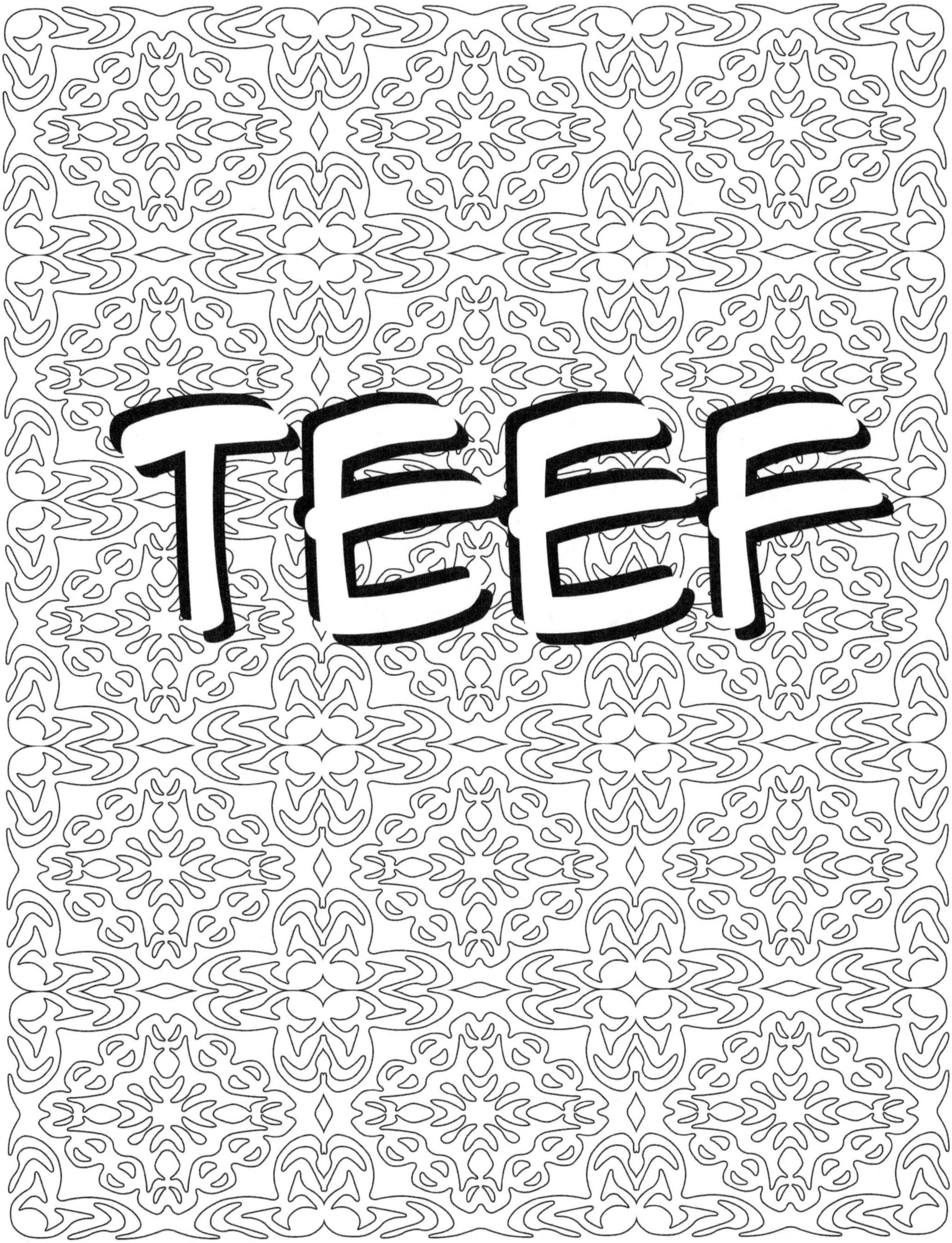
TEEF

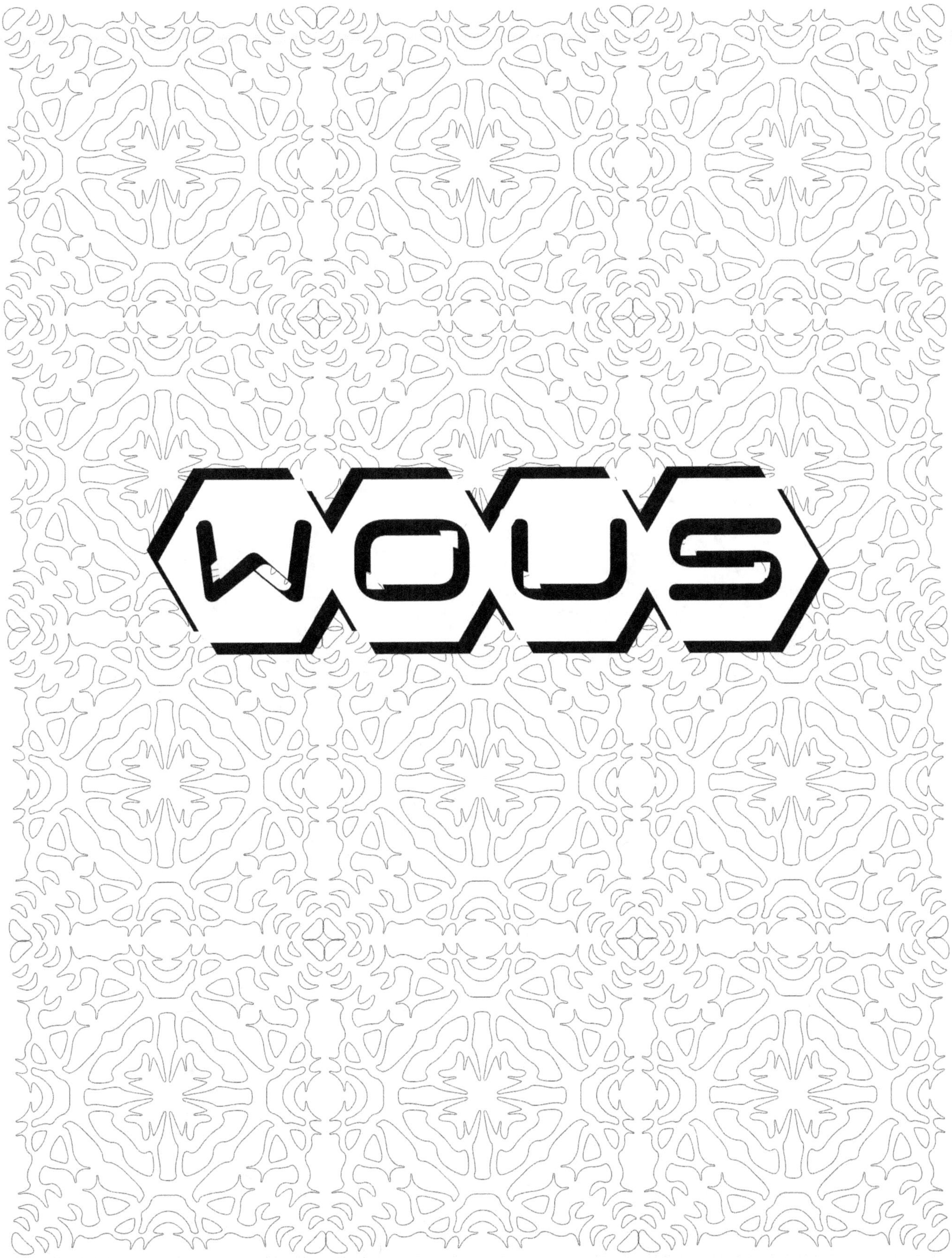
WOUS

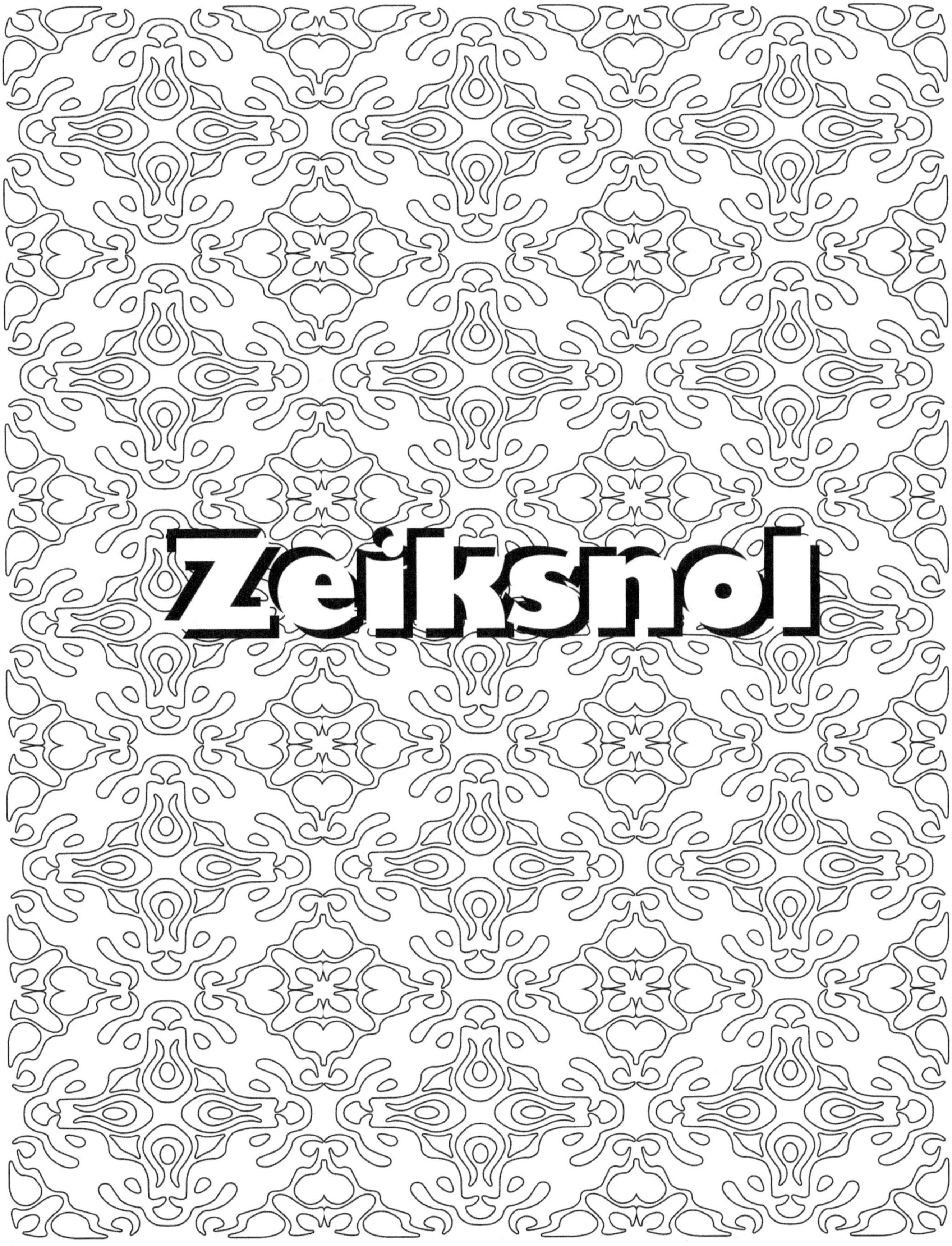
Zeiksnol

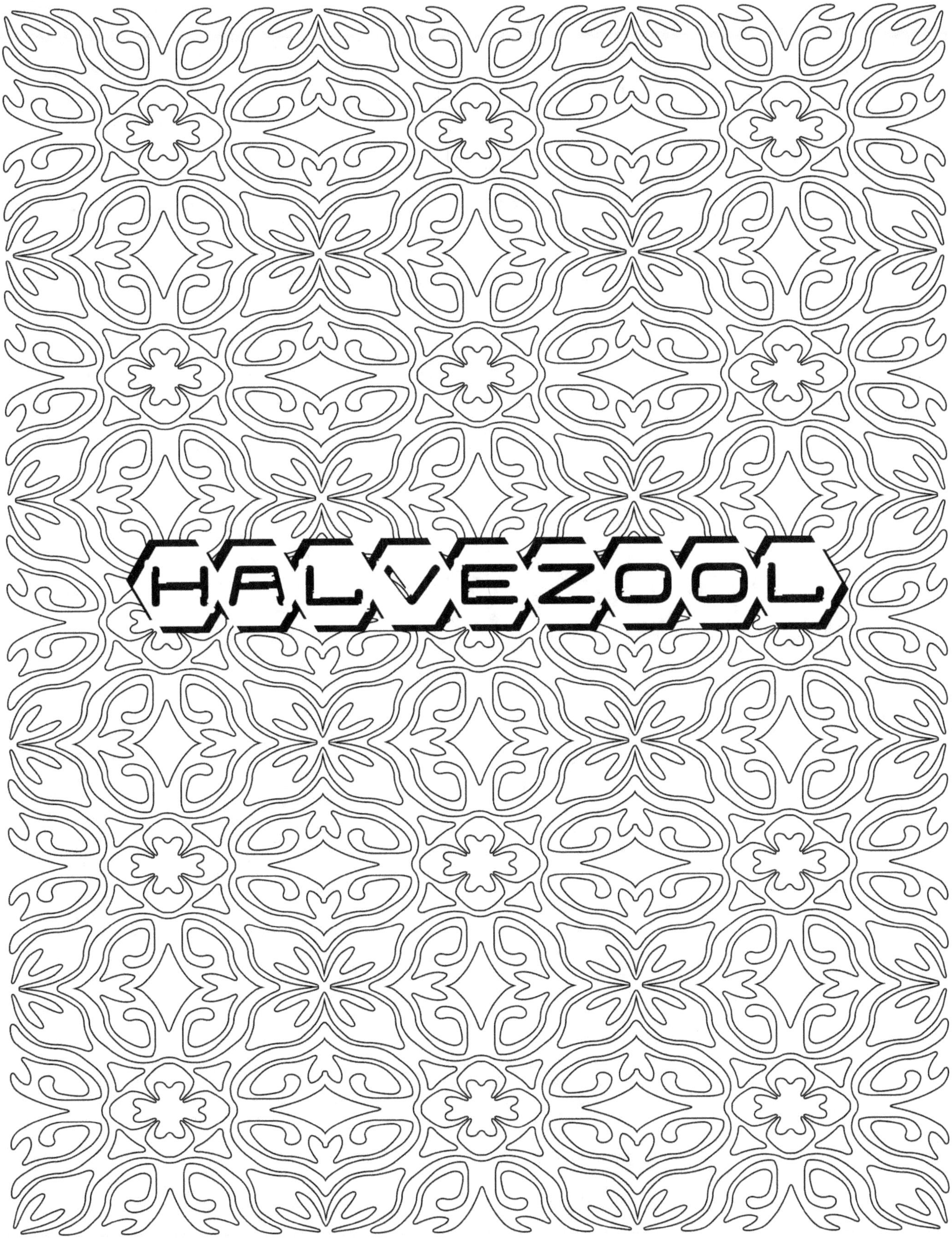
HALVEZOOL